'8

Images from the collections of Warrington Library,
Museum and Archive Service

WARRINGTON AT WORK

Images from the collections of Warrington Library,
Museum and Archive Service

WARRINGTON AT WORK

Janice Hayes and Alan Crosby

WARRINGTON
BOROUGH
COUNCIL

breedon **books**
PUBLISHING

First published in Great Britain in 2003 by
The Breedon Books Publishing Company Limited
Breedon House, 3 The Parker Centre,
Derby, DE21 4SZ.

ISBN 1 85983 365 9

Printed and bound by Butler & Tanner,
Frome, Somerset, England.

Cover printing by Lawrence-Allen Colour Printers,
Weston-super-Mare, Somerset, England.

Contents

Acknowledgements

Warrington At Work has been compiled from official records in numerous public and company archives; from images taken by professional and amateur photographers and from the family albums and reminiscences of Warrington workers themselves.

The majority of illustrations in this volume are from the extensive collection of images held by Warrington Library, Museum and Archive Service. The authors would like to thank staff past and present for their help and especially Heather McAlpine, Hilary Chambers, Keith Scott and Walter Simms, together with volunteers including Mike Dickinson, Les Johnson and Arthur Roberts.

The following organisations kindly gave permission for their archives to be used in *Warrington At Work*:

Images from the Stewart Bale collections on Pages 154-55 appear courtesy of the National Museums Liverpool (Merseyside Maritime Museum).

Ineos Silicas & Crosfield Archives appear on Pages 32, 48 and 142-151.

Archives of Stoves Ltd featuring Fletcher, Russell & Co and Richmonds appear on Pages 55, 58 and 131-4

150 years of reporting by the *Warrington Guardian* newspaper provided an invaluable resource of editorials, interviews and images.

Interviews including Joyce Lister, Frank McKie and Peter Spilsbury were compiled as part of the Heritage Lottery funded "A Gateway Through Time Project."

The memories of Mrs Bradley, Mrs Burke, Mrs Cash, Jim Coyne, Harry Hardman, Amy Pridden and Arthur Shelmerdine were recorded by the Warrington Workshop for Voluntary Action.

Special thanks are also due to all those who patiently contributed to the oral and written histories credited elsewhere in this volume and to members of the Latchford History Group and the Loushers Lane Memories Group.

This volume would not have been possible without the particular contribution of the photographers who have documented the working lives of Warrington people. Every effort has been made to trace the copyright holders but the Museum and Archive Service would be interested to learn of further details or sources of the images featured.

Setting the Scene

I
F YOU had asked any informed outsider 100 years ago what Warrington meant to them, their answer might have been 'wire, soap and beer'. Ask the great-great-great-grandchild of that outsider today, and the answer would probably be 'IKEA, new offices, maybe Persil...and probably Warrington Wolves'. This apparently changing picture of the town is the theme of *Warrington at Work*, which takes a wide-ranging and varied look at Warrington and its working life over the past 200 years and tries to show how the lives of its people have been shaped by employment.

Industry has played a vital part in Warrington's heritage, but there is much more to the town than that. Long before it became a major industrial centre, Warrington was a town which thrived on commercial activity and the provision of services such as shops and the market, the professions and transport. There were always industries – small craft trades mainly – but they were not the dominant element in the town's economy. Then, in the mid-18th century, several of these smaller trades began to expand and Warrington shared in the great social and economic upheaval for which Victorian writers coined the familiar term 'Industrial Revolution'. That revolution transformed the face of northern England and created, in a most dramatic fashion, the first industrial nation. South Lancashire and north Cheshire became the workshop of the world, and at the geographical heart of that region was Warrington.

The town itself underwent enormous changes as new industries came, existing ones grew rapidly from backstreet workshops to sprawling factories, large numbers of migrants came to the town seeking work, and the landscape and environment were altered almost beyond recognition. By 1900 Warrington was, to almost every observer, an industrial town through and through – but to those who cared to look more closely it was clear that the old businesses, the commerce, retailing and services, were still there and indeed flourishing as never before.

Women take to the factory floor during World War One and signal an intention to join the world of work on their own terms.

Warrington at work in the 1950s: a typical scene on the production lines of industry at British Aluminium's Sheet Rolling section.

The market was rebuilt, shops spread along Bridge Street and Sankey Street, Palmyra Square was full of professional gentlemen living in large houses, and the town's role as a transport hub was of exceptional importance.

Today, because industry has contracted and been 'downsized' so widely across north-west England, the service aspect of the town's employment profile has emerged into the limelight once more. Indeed for many people today it is the dominant element.

Warrington At Work illustrates not only the hard labour of those who toiled on the factory floor but also the bustling world of market traders and shop workers, the newer role of professionals and public servants. Not least it recalls

the unsung activities of countless men, women and children who have made their contributions to the story of *Warrington At Work*.

Although we could not include every type of employment or local firm in this book we have tried to present a truly representative coverage. We use not only pictures and photographs to show the visual reality of work, but also show how people's own accounts, written and spoken, form a vital resource in helping to understand how employment was in the past and how it contrasts and compares with working life today.

Houghton's wireworkers pause in their labours early last century.

The Importance of Transport

Welcome to Warrington in 1897! This view of the substantial three-arched Victoria Bridge over the River Mersey at Warrington shows the industrial landscape which greeted travellers on the main north-south thoroughfare. A contemporary visitor observed that there were '147 factory chimneys emitting black smoke daily, Sundays only excepted. A perpetual smoke hangs over the city like a pall, through which the sunlight only occasionally penetrates'.

TRANSPORT and accessibility has been a key to the success of Warrington for 2,000 years. It has allowed the town to thrive even when neighbouring places have suffered severe economic problems and also explains much about the character, physical shape and life of the town. But transport was also an industry and a major employer in its own right and, though the nature of transport has changed, it remains a vital part of the economy.

Warrington lies at a point which, before the 20th century, was the lowest convenient crossing of the Mersey for road travellers and Warrington's bridge

focussed traffic from the whole region. From the early 18th century local manufacturers and industrialists were prepared to invest heavily in road improvements, sponsoring the development of turnpikes. These were privately-owned trusts which took over existing roads and upgraded them by widening and resurfacing. Between 1726 and the end of the 18th century Warrington evolved as a focal point on the regional turnpike network (and thus, eventually, the national system) with seven key routes leading to the bridge over the Mersey.

Road improvements generated a great deal of trade and business for the town and indirectly provided work for many Warrington people. From the early 18th century the national stagecoach network transformed long-distance travel, with scheduled regular services, running to a timetable and with recognised stops. Warrington was a key point on this network, one of the places where travellers could join or leave coaches and where overnight stays were taken. As a result Warrington market became one of the largest and busiest in the north-west, enjoying the trade brought by the excellent access, and it drew its business from a huge tract of countryside and smaller towns north and south of the river. It was not only the market which benefited. The shops were busy and the town's craftsmen gained from the passing trade.

There was also work on the roads themselves. As well as the labourers who did the dirty work, mending potholes, digging out ditches, shovelling gravel and cutting back hedges, there were many others in and around the town who relied upon roads for their business. Warrington had a well-developed network of carriers, who drove the HGV-equivalents of the time, slow and lumbering carts – laden with goods, parcels, livestock (and people who took a cheap and uncomfortable ride) – which plodded their way along main roads and lanes out from the town. They linked Warrington with neighbouring towns and cities, and with the rural communities on the way, and were part of a huge and little-appreciated network of such routes. They kept the Industrial Revolution going. In 1828 the official lists of carriers, who regularly travelled a certain route on a fixed day each week, showed that towards Wigan and down the Knutsford road at least five such carts a day made the journey, while others trundled, less frequently, along the

By 1900 the 20 foot-wide Victoria Bridge had proved inadequate for the increasing volume of road traffic and an 85 foot-wide replacement was built. The first section of the innovative new reinforced Warrington Bridge is seen here under construction in 1913. "There is not a single improvement in Warrington which is more urgently needed... and everybody has been crying out for a new bridge for years," declared Alderman Bennett who had masterminded the project. Despite the construction of the motorways bypassing the town, and the construction of a second river crossing at Bridge Foot in the 1990s, Warrington Bridge is still a traffic bottleneck today as Warrington continues to play a vital role in the transport network.

roads to Birmingham, North Wales and Stoke-on-Trent. Unquestionably, many
other carriers operated less formally but no less frequently – a farmer in, say,
Burtonwood would go to Warrington market every week and as well as taking his
own produce might convey packages and parcels and pick up goods for local
people, in exchange for a few pence.

Despite the importance of Warrington's road network it was the town's water
and rail links which played a major role in the development of its economy.
Industry came to Warrington in the late 17th century and 200 years later, at the
height of Lancashire's golden age, the town was one of the leading industrial
centres. It had achieved this position despite two very obvious weaknesses. First,
it had no raw materials of the sort which usually help to explain Victorian industrial development: no stone, coal, iron ore, or minerals. Second, it had no power
source: the absence of coal and the lack of suitable streams for major water-
powered industries were serious deficiencies. The raw materials for the earliest
industries were the products of local agriculture – skins and hides supporting a
thriving leather industry; malt and grain for the brewing which was already
important in the early 18th century; and locally-grown flax and hemp providing
the linen and canvas yarns used in clothmaking and, in particular, the manufacture of sailcloth. Later industries exploited raw materials brought in from much
further afield by water (such as the copper ores from Anglesey and Cornwall
smelted at Bank Quay) and coal which was shipped to Warrington in barges from
St Helens and Worsley. The railway network, though, made possible large-scale
importing of coal and raw materials and in the mid-19th century, after rail access
opened up this greater potential, Warrington became a major industrial centre.

Employment in the transport sector grew very rapidly from the late 1830s
onwards and the figures from the 1891 census reveal the importance of this work

in the economy of the town. In that year the railways employed 480 people directly, and another 460 were engaged in road transport (compare these with the 95 who worked in water transport on canal and river shipping). But another 363 were involved in portering, or served as errand boys and messengers.

Furthermore, significant numbers were also engaged in ancillary trades, most notably the 125 in carriage, bicycle and vehicle building and repair. In total, the transport industry employed almost 1400 people in Warrington and, after metalworking, textiles, and domestic service, it was the town's largest employer. And these statistics just predate the advent of a further dimension to transport – in 1902 the borough council opened the first

tramway routes and a public transport system (entirely absent in 1891) developed, with further important opportunities for employment. The importance of transport is of course much greater even than any simple statistics suggest, for without the railway engine drivers, the porters, the shunters, the plate-layers, the carters and the wagon-drivers, Warrington's other vital industries would immediately have come to a standstill. The transport workers of Warrington kept the town and its economy going.

After 1945 the position changed quickly and fundamentally. Railways declined dramatically in relative significance as freight traffic shifted to the road vehicles and passengers to their cars. Several local lines saw passenger traffic disappear and, by the 1960s, freight services were going as well. But employment in the transport industry did not shrink. A new sector emerged – the long-distance lorry drivers, coach companies, taxi services and garages meant that the figures remained stable even if the industry was restructured almost beyond recognition. The express parcel firms and pizza delivery vans of today are the successors of the private carriers and carters of two centuries ago, while the long-distance coaches replicate – often down to the routes themselves – the stage-coaches of the 18th century. The message remains the same: transport, and those who work in it, are essential to the economic well-being of the town and the daily lives of its citizens.

In the 1830s the yard of the old Lion Inn off Bridge Street was the scene of frantic activity as the London-bound Royal Mail coach thundered in for a brief halt, as Robert Davies recalled: "When the coach drew up, there was a wild scuffle; men unharnessed each one of the smoking team, a man to a horse; another unbuckled the reins, leaving each horse to find its way to the stable yard; four other men were ready with the fresh horses. There was tallow thrust into the grease boxes, often buckets of water were thrown over the wheels, and the reins thrown up to the coachman. In moments the horses were in a canter, sometimes bucking and jumping, for they had had as much corn as they could get through, and the coach was quickly out of sight."

Staff of the Lower Seven Stars Inn in Lower Bridge Street proudly present one of the livestock taking advantage of the 'Good Stabling' to be found in the rear yard. One reason for the remarkable number of public houses and small hotels which formerly lined Bridge Street and the Market Gate area was the huge amount of business which the coaches brought. For hundreds of Warringtonians working life in the late 18th and early 19th centuries was spent in the stables and coach yards looking after the transport, or serving in the inns themselves. It was big business because, as well as the scheduled public coaches, there were also countless private journeys by coach and wagon and horse. Places such as Warrington were the motorway service stations and motels of their era and traffic continued day and night. Travellers demanded meals and drinks, beds, fodder and a place for the horses, running repairs to their vehicles, porters and grooms – all work for the people of the town.

The development of river and canal transport paralleled the expansion of the turnpikes and the two modes of transport were complementary, so that goods were transhipped from road to water and vice versa. Here employees of the Penketh Tannery unload hides at Fiddlers Ferry for the final leg of the journey by road.

'Warrington may in some measure be considered as a port town,'
wrote Aikin in 1795. Baines Directory of 1825 recorded: 'At the
time of the spring tides, the Mersey rises from 10 to 12 feet at
Warrington Bridge and vessels from 70 to 100 tons burden can
navigate the river to this point. The communication between
Manchester and Liverpool, by means of this navigation, is incessant, and the brick dust coloured sails of the barges are seen every
hour of the day on their passage, flickering on the wind.' In the
1950s firms such as the Bishop's Wharf Carrying Company,
Faircloughs Mills and Crosfield's still used the river to transport
raw materials and manufactured goods. Here Nathaniel Hough
sails his barge on one of Warrington's waterways.

A busy scene at London Bridge at Stockton Heath in 1908 as goods are unloaded from the barges for onward travel by horse and cart. The Bridgewater Canal had remained a busy goods highway despite the coming of the railways and improvements to road transport. This narrow bridge would be replaced in 1936 as the road was widened and the canal was later left to pleasure craft.

In the 20th century the building of the regional motorway network gave Warrington a nodal place on key national routes. The M6, M62 and M56, neatly boxing the town in, not only make it possible for long-distance traffic to avoid the centre, but also allow people to reach Warrington from far afield to take advantage of its commercial, retailing and office facilities. The motorways, like the muddy rutted roads of the 13th century, give Warrington unrivalled accessibility and its post-1960s boom has been made possible by their construction.

Breaking the ice at Stockton Heath in the early 1900s. Even the extremes of weather could not be allowed to close this still busy waterway.

The canals had tended to specialise in low-value bulk commodities such as coal and lime, while the roads were generally used for lighter traffic. By the time of this photograph in the early 1960s this coal-carrying flat boat was an increasingly rare sight on the Bridgewater Canal near Walton Bridge.

The canal network had bypassed Warrington – the Sankey Navigation, busy with coal from St Helens, came no nearer than Bewsey and Great Sankey, while the Bridgewater Canal was away on the Cheshire side at Stockton Heath. This encouraged a limited amount of commercial development (especially at the wharves at Latchford, Stockton Heath and Walton, where there were timber yards, coal yards and warehouses) but the canals always remained a relatively minor element in transport employment. The Manchester Ship Canal did, however, bring a good deal of industrial development and in the years after 1900 several large firms located new factories on the bank of the canal at Latchford.

By the 1830s the canal network was giving way to a new dominant form of transport the 'iron road' or the railway. This view from Roscoe's Book of the Grand Junction Railway *shows a canal barge (left) dwarfed by the splendid new 'Twelve Arches' railway viaduct at Walton.*

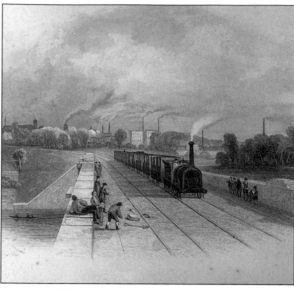

By the late 1830s the Grand Junction Railway had arrived at Bank Quay. Here this early locomotive gives a farewell puff of steam as it leaves behind the belching factory chimneys of a newly industrialised Warrington. Within 50 years Warrington factories would benefit from the completion of local links to the national railway networks.

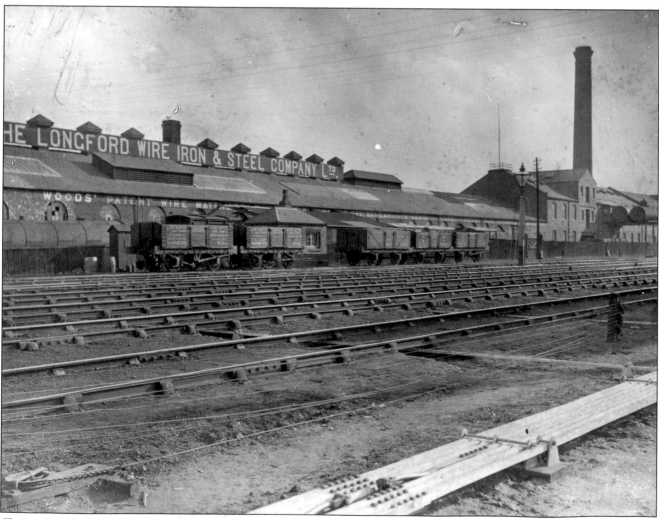

The Longford Wire Iron and Steel Company was just one of many Warrington firms to locate itself near to a major railway line. Rylands wireworks had its own sidings on the Cheshire Line at its Battersby Lane works whilst Crosfield's had both river and rail links at Bank Quay.

1	Longford Gasworks	12	Sankey Wire	23	Thomas Board Mills
2	USAF Burtonwood	13	Mersey White Lead	24	Fletcher Russell
3	A. Monk	14	John Clare Shipwrights	25	Wharf
4	N. Greening and Sons	15	Monks Hall Steelworks	26	Lion Emulsions
5	Pearson and Knowles	16	Mersey Flint Glassworks	27	Greenall Whitley
6	Walker Brewery	17	Bishops Wharf	28	Foundry
7	Cheshire Lines Workshops	18	Fairclough's Mill	29	Richard Evans and Company
8	Rylands Brothers	19	Howley Quay	30	Laporte Chemicals
9	Whitecross Company	20	Crosfields	31	Wharf
10	Crosfields	21	Crosfields		
11	Liverpool Refrigeration	22	British Aluminium		

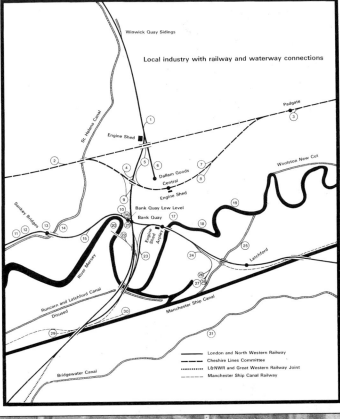

Railway pioneer William Allcard (1801-61) was appointed a Chief Engineer on the Liverpool to Manchester Railway by George Stephenson and drove the Comet *at the opening in 1830. Heavily involved in the construction of the Grand Junction Railway, linking Warrington to Birmingham, Allcard went into partnership with William Buddicom to build locomotives. He also built carriages in a factory behind Bank House off Sankey Street where he lived from 1839-1854.. He was twice mayor of Warrington before retiring to his native Derbyshire.*

Warrington railway workers took part in the National Railway Strike of 18-19 August 1911 during a time of massive industrial unrest. The railway workers went on strike in August 1911 to demand an increase in pay of 2s (10p) a week and a 54-hour week instead of 60 hours. A national state of emergency was declared and at Warrington 336 men and 15 officers of the 18th Hussars were sent to guard railway property and ensure the movement of essential supplies.

Staff at Bank Quay station pose for the camera in the early 20th century. As a leading industrial centre Warrington was a major traffic source for the railway network, while its position on the two trunk routes from London to Scotland and Liverpool to Manchester meant that its two stations were large and busy, served by numerous staff. It is often forgotten how labour-intensive the railway industry was until technological changes, shifting traffic patterns, and extensive 'downsizing' drastically reduced employee numbers from the early 1950s onwards. Even the smallest station had several staff, while those as busy as Bank Quay employed small armies. To work for a railway company in the golden age of railways meant a certain 'quality', a status in the community which was much sought after.

The railway delivery horses at Warrington's Central Station enjoyed a rare rest day during the National Railway Strike of August 1911.

Many of the town's industries were served by their own private railway sidings, but for the others a fleet of delivery vehicles, owned by the railway companies or industrial firms, collected goods from stations and yards and delivered them to the works, or took the finished products for onward shipment by rail. Through the busy streets of the town, each day, these horse-drawn carts and wagons (and, from the early years of the 20th century, steam or motor lorries) maintained an intensive service of local freight traffic.

Many Warrington firms continued to use horse-drawn wagons well into the 20th century and here Mr Holt and his charge stand poised to deliver another heavy load from Whitecross works.

The coalman with his horse and cart was still a familiar sight around Warrington's back streets in the 1950s. Here the local weights and measures inspectors check one of the sacks of coal for short weight.

An unexpected downpour gave a whole new meaning to the term 'milk float' as this Latchford milkman made his daily deliveries in the 1950s.

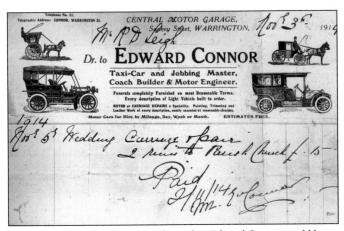

By 1914 the time was fast approaching when Edward Connor would have to decide whether to finally abandon his long-established horse-drawn carriage business for the horseless carriage. In 1897 his new premises in Sankey Street were described thus: 'A model of organisation and equipment... including telephonic communications. Every vehicle is sent out in perfect order down to the smallest detail, while none but specially picked men are employed in any department, and only thoroughly capable, civil and trustworthy men are allowed out in charge of the vehicles... A special department for funeral furnishing and undertaking includes horses, elegant mourning coaches, hearses and model funeral cars'.

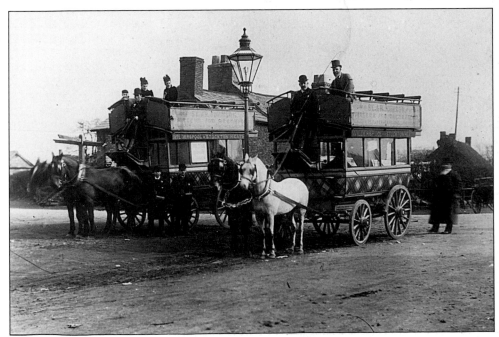

Intrepid travellers from Stockton Heath to Warrington town centre in 1900 were still reliant on these horse-drawn omnibuses, which bore more than a passing resemblance to the stage coaches of the American Wild West.

By the turn of the 20th century the age of the horse was slowly giving way to the era of the internal combustion engine. This photograph show one of Warrington's last annual horse-fairs which were held in Winwick Street near to the entrance of Central Station. In 1894 the Warrington Guardian urged the end of this traditional event: 'The cattle and horse fairs were held this week as usual... It was a public disgrace to the town to hold such fairs in the public streets of Warrington, for the filth in the streets in consequence was simply disgusting... A person unacquainted with Warrington, passing along the Cheshire Lines Railway would almost fancy he was passing an old world town when he saw the cattle and horses put up for sale in the streets. It is getting time that a more suitable place was provided so that the dealers can carry on their trade without being a nuisance to the public.'

The Cemetery to Bridge Street omnibus had room for few passengers but few working people could afford the fare of one old penny. Edward Connor's firm had the monopoly of the privately-operated horsebus routes in Warrington but this trade was lost with the introduction of Warrington Borough Council's tramway service from 1902.

In the years just before World War One a smart young chauffeur proudly poses with his employer's gleaming new motor car. Barely a decade earlier he might well have been grooming two glossy horses and driving the family's private carriage.

The Fairfield Motor Company of Padgate Lane not only operated a private-hire charabanc but also rather daringly ran a taxi service driven by a woman.

W. H. Bellian, noted coachbuilder and cycle manufacturer, had boldly branched out by opening this car and cycle showroom at 115 Sankey Street.

By 1926 the motor car was becoming a more familiar sight on Warrington streets and Garland's splendid car showrooms in Bridge Street represented one of the new breed of transport workers – car salesmen.

Warrington Motor Company's splendid Art Deco car showrooms were ready to put the new 8 horse-power Ford through its paces in a '72-hour continuous non-stop run'.

The traditional occupations of coachbuilders, wheelwrights and upholsterers found new employment in the transport industry. The delivery vehicles produced by Marsdens were a far cry from the old horse-drawn equivalents but the company continued to trade as 'coachbuilders'.

A rare interior shot inside Spann's body building workshop off Bold Street. As the workmen put the finishing touches to a variety of vehicles a new trailer for Rylands wireworks is awaiting collection.

Staff at Bennett's Cake works proudly pose with their fleet of delivery vans. John Jones (extreme right, back row) was the first salesman to be employed by Bennett's Confectionery. He had delivered cakes in his horse-drawn van to shops in Warrington and as far afield as Runcorn and Widnes.

Bill Rutter, who worked for Greenall's Brewery for over 40 years, had fond memories of some of his delivery lorries and revealed the complexities of his job: "By the time I left the company I had driven more than two million miles, going as far north as Glasgow, Edinburgh and Stranraer and south to London Eastbourne and Cornwall. In the Midlands I'd drive to Nottingham, Birmingham, Oxford and across to Hull in the North-East and other places too numerous to mention. Working on transport you needed to be able to adapt very quickly to a great variation of gear boxes... Some of them had a two-speed back axle, while others had splitter boxes. To drive a splitter box, say on a 10-speed, you would drive through the first five then split the box by shifting a lever at the top of the gear stick. This would then put you into high range, from low range, then you go through the same five positions making them into 6, 7, 8, 9 and 10. It kept you on your toes! Some wagons were given nicknames. One particular wagon had a habit of spluttering. This wagon was given the name of 'Farting Fan'. Very apt."

Location, Location, Location

Here a Warrington black-smith is hard at work in the early years of the 20th century when areas of Warrington were still rural and the horse was still an essential part of daily life.

BEFORE the age of the commuter Warrington people lived, in some cases literally, on top of the workshops and backyard industries. The clanging sound of hammers and the rasping of saws, the wheezing of bellows fanning the flames of hearths, the smell of newly-cut wood, or coke and charcoal fumes, were part of everyday life.

Warrington's earliest industries were located in and around the medieval centre, in workshops and backyards. The small scale of activity, and location close to or among housing areas, is very typical of most towns in the 17th and early 18th centuries. Even in the first decades of the 20th century plenty of examples of backyard workshops could be found in the town, employing just one or two people. Typical of the trades in such places were the carpenters, black-smiths, wheelwrights, wagon-makers, and clogmakers, all the specialised crafts which were found in just about every town and village.

There were, however, certain other crafts and backyard industries more specific to south Lancashire and to the Warrington area in particular. Among these were pinmaking, the making of hand tools and numerous other small

and specialised metal items such as the links of chains, locks and bolts, or watch and clock parts. The town eventually achieved a dominant position in the hand tool and pin industries, but the pattern of small trades established continued – pinmaking, for example, was always a workshop-based business, right up to the time it disappeared in the 1870s and 1880s. Making hand tools, although increasingly concentrated in Peter Stubs' great Scotland Road works at Cockhedge, remained, in part, a small workshop trade into the later 19th century.

Employees of Ferguson's forge and veterinary practice in Suez Street in the 1890s still work in the heart of Warrington town centre.

There was another, quite different, industrial area by the middle of the 19th century – the riverside. The medieval town mills were at Howley, where the Mersey Mills stood on the north bank of the river and were fed by a millrace which cut across the neck of the bend just below Howley footbridge. Other watermills were on side streams, such as the Sankey cornmill which was approximately where Sacred Heart RC School is today. The improvement of the river for navigation up to Warrington in the 1690s, and above Warrington to Manchester in the 1720s and 1730s, encouraged further industrial development. A great diversity of industries appeared along the north bank between Atherton's Quay (off Liverpool Road opposite Beaufort Street) and Bank Quay. The building of the railway past Bank Quay in the 1840s and the line through Arpley and Sankey a decade later reinforced the importance of this industrial zone and led to major expansion of the soapworks and iron and steel works. The eventual result was the large and dominating complex of the Unilever works just next to Bank Quay station. Meanwhile other workshops and warehouses were built at Bishop's Wharf next to the town bridge.

Elsewhere, Victorian industries expanded on the undeveloped land at the

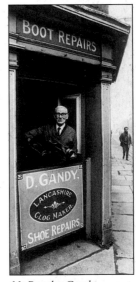

Mr Douglas Gandy, Warrington's last clogmaker, poses outside his shop in Mersey Street about 1970. As wages rose clogs fell out of fashion to be replaced by rubber-soled working boots.

edge of the old town. The larger scale and more ambitious 'production lines' of industrial concerns after the 1840s meant that more spacious sites with plenty of room for expansion were essential, while the need to bring in large quantities of coal for steam-power and to transport the finished product gave a special advantage to sites close to the rail network. The problem for many of these mid-19th century industrial plants was that although they were on greenfield sites when established, the growth of the town soon surrounded them with streets and houses so that the potential for expansion was lost. Thus the Rylands wireworks in Church Street (which was founded in 1817 but grew rapidly from 1843 onwards), the Armitage and Rigby cotton mills at Cockhedge, and the Winwick Street tanneries all backed on to open land when they were developed but by 1900 were deep within the built-up area. Even the new generation of tanneries built on the riverside at Howley from the 1860s onwards encountered these problems.

During the 20th century industrial development continued to move further away from the old town and the existing built-up area, as new locations were opened up. Thus the Greenall's brewery complex expanded across the flat river-

As the era of the horse gave way to the age of the internal combustion engine traditional blacksmiths had to find new employment in firms like Crosfield's or the town's foundries and metal works.

side lands at Wilderspool; industrial estates were laid out in places such as Woolston, Hawleys Lane and alongside the canal at Baronet Lane; and the small industries and out of date and cramped premises closer to the centre gradually succumbed to structural changes in industry, town planning and renewal schemes, and a general policy of segregating industry from housing and commercial areas. By 1970, when the plans for the redevelopment of the old town were being drawn up, many of the 18th and 19th century industrial buildings – the workshops and backyard warehouses – had already vanished. Twenty years later hardly any remained. Great swathes of industrial Warrington were flattened and redeveloped and in most instances it is hard to find any trace of what were, for 200 years, small factories, workshops and even large industrial concerns. Who, 50 years ago, could have imagined that Rylands in Church Street would simply disappear, to be replaced by a supermarket and its sprawling acres of car park?

Today, when we look at the location of employment in the borough of Warrington, we see how the trend towards moving to the periphery has continued. The plans for the new town, implemented from the late 1960s onwards, emphasised the creation of major new employment areas on the outskirts of the town, close to motorway junctions and major urban expressways. Although new industrial areas were included within the expansion scheme, much of the employment increase was always intended to be in the service sector – offices, retailing, research and development, and transport – and this has been the case to an even greater extent than the original planning strategy anticipated. Though Warrington still has an important industrial sector, the percentage of its workforce employed in industry is now lower than at any time in the past 200 years.

Amongst the more unusual small workshops which were crammed into Warrington's town centre was that of the Jolley family of Bank Street who had since 1885 produced cat-gut to string violins. Here Mr .W.R Jolley winds the cat-gut (actually lamb intestines) on to a frame to dry. As the Warrington Examiner *reporter revealed: 'Guts are peculiar things to handle. The layman might just as well try to hold a very lively eel'. To the Jolleys it was all part of a day's work but it was hardly an ideal occupation in the summer months when 'Mr Jolley works in a room with a window closed, the door padded, and a roaring fire thrusting the mercury in the thermometer up to 111 degrees....necessary if the gut is to be perfect and dried'.*

The clatter of wooden soles on cobblestones and the sparks from the clog irons were a traditional part of working life in the early 20th century. Houghton's clogmaking workshop off Buttermarket Street demonstrates the volume of clogs once produced to provide sturdy long-lasting footwear which protected workers in many industries. Houghton's was virtually an assembly line for clogs. In the background are the shaped alder wood soles bought in from a clogger. Leather uppers were stretched over the different sized wooden lasts (seen in the box in the foreground) and held in place by metal studs which were tapped in by a small clogging hammer. Meanwhile another group of workers fixed the metal clog irons on to the soles.

This view of the River Mersey from Knutsford Road in the 1790s shows the Howley Mill and the old Parish Church on the right. In the foreground men are netting shoals of sparlings, just one of the catches to be had in Warrington's former fishing industry. The Universal Directory *of 1792 recorded: 'In the river are caught sturgeons, greenbacks, mullets, sand eels, lobsters, shrimps, prawns, and the best and largest cockles in all of England.' Overfishing and the growth of industry along the river banks had killed off the trade within another 50 years.*

Although the fishermen had disappeared, the River Mersey at Howley was still being used by barges in the middle of the 20th century.

By the time of this engraving in 1772, Bank Quay was becoming established as an industrial centre and also a port before Liverpool took over this regional role. A steady stream of flat-bottomed boats brought their cargoes to the warehouses on the quay side. On the left are the two cones of the Bank Quay glass houses whilst the chimneys of Thomas Patten's copper-smelting works can be seen between the sails of the central two boats. This and other business interests had brought him sufficient wealth to commission leading architect James Gibbs to build him a new mansion which rose above the river. Known then as Bank Hall, it is better known nowadays as Warrington's Town Hall.

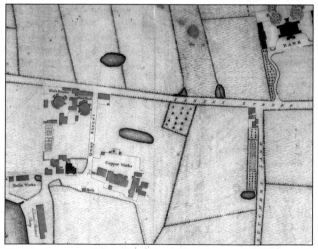

The development of Bank Quay can clearly be seen on Donbavand's map of 1772.

A comparison with this 1826 map of Bank Quay shows the rapid industrial development of the site. The glassworks had expanded, Crosfield's had opened their soapery near the river and, to the right of the glassworks, a cotton factory, with adjacent workers' housing, had also appeared.

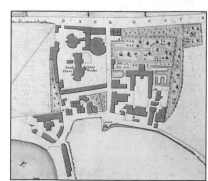

This photograph of Bank Quay taken in the late 1870s shows raw materials being unloaded, probably for Crosfield's works. This site was still known as the Pottery Wharf after a short-lived experiment of the early 19th century when James and Fletcher Bolton had attempted to establish a potteryworks at there. Choosing the site because Cornish clay could be shipped up river from Liverpool the brothers set up a works run by a pupil of Josiah Wedgwood. A colony of potters and their families were transported by canal from Staffordshire to settle in the newly-built cottages of Potters Yard. The immigrants kept apart from the locals and used their expertise to produce a variety of pottery for the American market. Disaster struck in 1807 when, in an attempt to prevent the warring British and French navies from interfering with neutral US trading ships, the American President Thomas Jefferson banned the import of all European-made goods; the firm went bankrupt and the workers went back to Staffordshire. The site itself would later be taken over in the 1850s by Tayleurs for the building of iron ships.

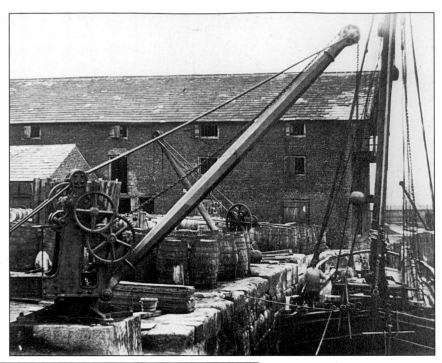

This view of Bank Quay in the 1890s shows the development of Crosfield's site to the right, whilst a single cone of Robinson's new glass-works is visible in the background. In the centre is Fairclough's Bank Quay Mill. They were the last firm to transport their goods by barges, only ceasing operation in 1984.

By the early 1900s Crosfield's soapworks dominated at Bank Quay, exploiting an excellent transport network of river traffic and private railway sidings, linked to the nearby main line. To the right of the photograph is the transporter bridge which provided a link to their operations on the Cheshire side of the river.

A second major quayside, known as Bishop's Wharf, had developed near to Warrington Bridge to serve the industries at Howley. Here the Bishop's Wharf Carrying Company offered 'a regular service between Warrington and Liverpool by fleet of new-built steel barges'. They specialised in handling hides and other raw materials for the numerous Warrington tanneries. In 1933 the Warrington Examiner hailed Bishop's Wharf as 'Prosperity Corner' and the home of various trades. Here the explorer would 'smell strange smells'. The article went on: 'The curious odour of molten iron, the smell of hot rubber, the sharp tang of hides in pickle, the rich, dry smell of grain. He will hear the merry rattle of chains and the thud of grain sacks, the impatient throb of laden motor-lorries and the laboured tread of patient dray horses. Tied up to the wharf itself are business like stout little river boats into whose capacious holds donkey engines drop load upon load of Warrington wire that shines like new silver, and bags of nails, making the lumbering, honest-looking craft strain against their ropes.'

By the late 1950s Bishop's Wharf was a much quieter place. Soon the last of Warrington's tanneries would close whilst the site itself would eventually be redeveloped as the Riverside Retail Park.

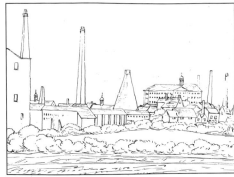

Cockhedge in the early 1830s still seems an almost rural location but industrialisation was fast encroaching. In the background the bell tower of the cotton factory calls the spinners and weavers who have had to relocate from the surrounding countryside. Nearby is the cone of the Cockhedge crown glassworks rising above a huddle of workers' houses and other small work places.

An aerial photograph of the Cockhedge area in the early 1930s reveals a completely industrial landscape. In the foreground Buttermarket Street curves along the bottom of the picture to be intersected by Scotland Road, with Peter Stubs' fileworks on the right. In the background is the major transport artery of the Cheshire Lines Railway with its dominant warehouse. To the right of the warehouse are the towering chimney of Armitage & Rigby's Cotton Mill, with the white reflected light from the glass roof tops of the weaving sheds. Interspersed amongst other smaller workshops are the workers' cottages which live cheek-by-jowl with the heavy industry.

The Ordnance Survey maps of 1850-51 show that in several areas immediately outside the town centre – including Tanners Lane and Winwick Street – tanneries occupied cramped sites immediately adjacent to areas of poor housing. When some of these tanneries were established in the early 18th century they lay on the edge of the town, but housing and commercial development rapidly surrounded them so that, by 1850, they were embedded within the built-up area. Tanneries were particularly obnoxious, because they gave off a vile stench. The flesh, fat and hair which adhered to the hides and skins had to be rotted off in pits of caustic solutions, producing not only an intolerable smell but also a serious risk of water pollution.

This rented housing off Winwick Street was typical of the crowded insanitary conditions experienced by most of the working-class in the earlier 20th century. A reporter from the Warrington Examiner *newspaper* described his findings in 'Slumland':

'The wife is a cleanly, decent woman, doing her best to keep a large family together on a moderate income. But as she says quite openly, it is difficult to keep anything clean with the smuts constantly falling from the large works nearby. She confesses how the smell from the pail closet, which is within two yards of her back door penetrates within the house and when the weather is at all warm, makes her feel "swimming inside".

'There are three small children [and] the only place where they can play is out in the backyard. By some Dispensation of Providence, so far these children have survived, but naturally they are stunted in form and the eldest show signs of tubercular trouble. No wonder for every foul liquid imaginable must have fallen into that backyard and later in the form of dust, defiled those children's insides. The water arrangements of the house are just as primitive as the sanitary arrangements There is only one tap and that is in the front room and, if not turned off, it drips on to the floor and constitutes a damp breeding place for germs. Innumerable flies feast and batten upon the plentiful corruption provided around the house and carry their little load of microbes into the food, the children's milk and even the father's beer. Another little mortal is expected to arrive soon into this curious world of smells and dinginess and hard conditions. The poor little beggar will not stand much of a chance.

'Within the walls of that little house are contained practically every social problem which exists today – unemployment, housing, feeding, sanitary conditions, tuberculosis and so forth... By sheer force of economics these people are compelled to live in such lodgings as the landlord provides. Of course, there is money wasted on drink and so forth even in some of the poorest households... Many have never had a fair chance. Many have never known what it is to live in houses which are clean and fresh.'

Employment in Warrington 1891 and 2003

BY THE end of the 19th century Warrington was reaching its peak as an industrial centre. Manufacturing had its largest share of employment and the industrial diversity of the town was at its greatest. The detailed structure of employment can be discovered by using the census returns, which in the late Victorian period give copious statistics about the workforce of every town with over 50,000 people. In 1891 Warrington came within that category for

The weaving shed at Cockhedge in the early 20th century is filled with a predominantly female labour force, with authority figures represented by the two male chargehands. However, the more experienced weavers could earn a good wage, even more than their husbands who worked elsewhere in industry.

the first time and in the published census volumes of that year we have a clear picture of how many men and women were employed in which trades and jobs. We can see which trades were the town's largest employers and identify differences between the work done by men and women. It is very illuminating to look at this picture of Warrington in the last years of Victoria's reign and to compare it with the Warrington of today. The differences are remarkable, and they reflect the fundamental changes in the town during the past half century as traditional industries have crumbled and new work patterns have taken their place. The 1890s have other importance to historians of work in the town. It is from this date that large numbers of pictures become available, as amateur and professional photographers took their cameras into workshops, factories and business premises. And when, in the 1940s, the first detailed written reminiscences produced by ordinary people were published in local papers, the subjects looked back over half a century of work, change and upheaval to the 1890s when they started employment. Thereafter, in most of Warrington's major trades, we have recollections and oral history interviews to tell us what it was like. From the 1890s we begin to appreciate the reality of work and labour in a way which we simply cannot do for previous generations.

In 1891 female employment was dominated by two types of work. The most important was the textile industry, with over 2,500 women workers (almost all of whom were in the cotton and fustian trades). Thus, although Warrington was never a cotton town in the sense of, say, Oldham or Bolton, the industry was very

All was not quite as it seemed at Wood's sweet shop in Buttermarket Street, near to St Mary's Church. Father was actually employed as a postman whilst Mrs Wood was the brains behind the business, as well as raising the children.

Payton's shop in Church Street was typical of many small shops run from the front room of a terraced house, often by a woman supplementing the family income. Mrs Cash recalls her grandmother's shop at Orford: "This was in the front room which had a wide window. We had shelves and used some of the furniture, the side board and things for drawers. There was all home cooked stuff done in the range. Gran cooked and baked. There was cooked meats, roast heart, roast pork, savoury ducks. Well it kept us but we never made that much."

There were also opportunities for male domestic servants, especially on the country estates on Warrington's outskirts. Sir Gilbert Greenall employed a large staff of grooms, gardeners and estate workers as well as his male indoor servants at Walton Hall.

important. It accounted for over a third of all female employment in the town. Since other major industries, such as wiremaking and ironworking, traditionally employed very few women, the growth of the textile trade made a major difference to opportunities for women to find reasonably well-paid and secure work. The other essential area for women's labour in 1891 was domestic service. In that year 1,650 Warrington women were listed in this category (though a great many others were also engaged in domestic service but on a casual or part-time basis and do not appear in the figures). Over a quarter of female full-time jobs were in domestic service, mostly in private houses. Textiles and domestic service between them accounted for 67 per cent of all work for women in Warrington. Some other key areas where large numbers of women were employed were clothing (where women worked as seamstresses, milliners, and tailors); food dealing (grocery and other provision shops, and market stalls) and general shopkeeping; and teaching and education. It is striking that in 1891 very few women were employed in offices and clerical work – only eight women in the whole town worked in local government, for example – but the growth of this sector was to be one of the most impressive features of the next half century.

Employment for men was more evenly spread, and far more jobs were available. Only one-third of Warrington females over the age of 10 were at work in 1891, compared with 86 per cent of males. In a town with a lot of heavy industry (which was entirely a man's world) that was not unexpected, but far fewer Warrington women were able to find paid employment than in the cotton towns, where it was usual for 60-70 per cent of all women to have jobs. On the other hand, Warrington women had more opportunities than in towns such as St Helens and Widnes, where the dominance of industries such as glass and chemicals gave little chance of expanding the jobs for women. A feature of Warrington at work over the 20th century was the inexorable rise of female employment. By the 1960s it was commonplace for women to work and by the end of the 1990s more women were at work than men.

In the days before World War Two many young women found employment in domestic service, either as housemaids or working their way up the hierarchy in the kitchen to become the family cook. May Green recalls her weekly routine at Walton Hall: "I was 15 when I went to work in the kitchens, that would be about 1935. I did mostly the vegetables for the servants' hall and the dining room. I had to cook all the servants' hall breakfast and the housekeeper's room breakfast. Then we used to help Miss Musson, the cook making all the sauces and other kinds of things we had to do when all the family was at home. You had to get all the things ready for the oven, like grouse and all the game birds. I had to pluck all those as a scullery maid. They used to leave wild ducks until they were high, and I've seen the ducks moving from side to side because they were full of maggots... and they would eat them like that! "Another larder had great black stone slabs in it where they used to put things like fish to keep cold. Then there was the dairy where Mr. Rowe used to churn butter on Thursdays. They had cows down at the shippons near the bridge (where they put the toilets later.) The cows kept us in milk and butter and cream. Every Thursday morning before breakfast we had to clean all the copper things on the kitchen shelves. There were all sorts of things like jelly moulds and great big preserving pans."

Smaller households commonly employed at least one domestic servant. This rare early photograph from the 1860s is dated by the servant's surprisingly fashionable 'pork pie' hat. Otherwise there is a timeless quality as she performs her routine chore, carrying the traditional 'piggin' or wooden bucket, possibly made by the local cooper.

For men the largest single category of work in 1891 was what was described as 'mechanics and labourers' – in other words, the unskilled workforce which had no training, no specific job description, and simply dug, or shifted, or carried, or heaved, in all manner of trades and occupations. Almost 20 per cent of Warrington men were in this large, amorphous and poorly-paid group. They were followed by the iron industry, which perhaps unexpectedly was the largest single employer in the town, with 2,345 men listed in this category in the census. In fact, the statistics deceive. A lot of these men worked at Monks Hall, in the ironworks, but many others were employed in the foundries attached to the wireworks though they were not classified as wireworkers. Wiremaking itself (that is, the skilled trade of the wiredrawers and their teams) employed 1,036 people, but if the workers in the foundries and metalwork shops were added to the number we would find that wire was undoubtedly the town's leading industry. Metalworking of all types (ranging from smelting, ironfounding and casting through to wiredrawing) employed 15 per cent of the total Warrington workforce. That statistic is very significant. It emphasises how diverse and broad-based the town's economy was: in the cotton towns a single industry (and often one sector of that one industry – spinning, or weaving) typically accounted for 60 or more per cent of all employment. In Warrington, the largest single industry represented only 15 per cent of the workforce, textiles another 13 per cent, domestic service 7.5 per cent and clothing production and the building and construction trades just over 5 per cent each. For a north-western town this was a remarkably diverse (and hence outstandingly secure) employment structure.

There are other noteworthy features of the 1891 statistics. Perhaps the most improbable to us today is the small size of the public sector. It is astonishing to think that in 1891 there were only 38 people in the whole town engaged in the administration of local government (though others were employed by the borough council as labourers and there was a borough police force of 51 people including administrative clerks). Another very small sector, which would later grow more dramatically than any other, was finance and money. In 1891

By the period of World War One domestic service was beginning to fall out of favour as a lowly-paid occupation. Another opening for female employment occurred with the opening of laundries, like the Latchford laundry pictured here.

Warrington had just 20 people employed by banks, 69 in insurance (including door-to-door salesmen, a new occupation in late Victorian England) and 710 people of all levels engaged in 'business' as clerks, agents for shipping companies, import and export merchants and others in 'general trade'. Office employment was almost entirely confined to the administration of trades and industries – the white-collar workers who dealt with the paperwork in factories and businesses. The notion of office work in the pure sense – consultancies, management agencies, advertising and design – was far in the future.

So in 1891 industry was indeed dominant. Since then the changes in the employment structure have been dramatic, as the table below indicates. It shows the percentages in different categories of employment in 1891 and 1999 (the figures are approximations because frequent changes in the basis for calculating government statistics mean that direct comparisons cannot be made):

Category	1891	1999
agriculture, forestry and fishing	< 1%	1%
energy and water supplies	< 1%	4.8%
manufacturing	63.7%	16.5%
construction	5.1%	5.9%
retailing, distribution, catering, hotels etc	20.4%	27.1%
transport and communications	4.7%	7.1%
banking, finance and insurance	< 1%	20.6%
public sector including health and education	4.8%	17.1%

< = less than; figures do not add to 100 per cent because of rounding up

Thus, the shape of employment in Warrington has shifted in the past half century from a dominance by industry, manufacturing and production, the town's leading role for over a hundred years, to the preponderance of the service

By 1914 more women had found employment in the local factories where their long hair presented a potential hazard with machinery. Crosfield's issued their female employees with protective clothing which included sun-bonnets traditionally worn by agricultural workers. Crosfield's were known as good employers but they were also concerned to uphold family values. As a result women were compelled to give up their jobs when they married.

These women workers at Whitecross during World War One tackled some of the heavy work normally undertaken by men. Despite the agitation of the Suffragettes and the increased use of women workers in both world wars of the 20th century the struggle for equal pay took much longer to achieve. David recalls attitudes in the wire industry in the mid-1960s: "I was 17 and the women who were working around me, grown women of 35 were roughly on the same money I was on. All the men who were 21 earned about a third or a quarter more than the women. The unions came along and said: 'This has got to stop; equal pay for women,' which today sounds straightforward but then it wasn't. There was a mentality, like apartheid basically. Women didn't get the same and a lot of men were dead against equal pay. We came out on strike on the shop floor for equal pay for women. We lost pay and we couldn't afford to lose money in those days. The unions called a meeting in the offices and not one man turned up. They weren't having women being on the same rate of pay as them. It was their status they were bothered about. The dispute was right across the country for equal pay for women. It went on for a few years and then the Labour government brought it in. It made a big difference to women, women on the shop floor too."

Large scale engineering projects created plentiful employment for labourers like the navigators (or navvies) who descended on Warrington in the early 1890s with the building of the Manchester Ship Canal. This famous image of the navvies at Acton Grange was taken by local photographer Thomas Birtles and reveals the dangerous conditions in which they worked.

Shirt sleeves rolled up ready for action Houghtons' wire workers brace themselves for another hard shift. They are clad in their characteristic work clothes with only a rough sacking apron for protection.

sector and the provision of office jobs. Retailing, distribution and catering accounted for 20 per cent of jobs in the late 19th century and had only increased relatively modestly, to 27 per cent by the end of the 20th, though the actual numbers employed rose very rapidly. This essential stability reflects Warrington's continued regional role as a shopping centre and, in recent years, as a nationally-important focus for warehousing and distribution activities. It is a solid and dependable basis for the town's economy. The figures can be 'reshaped' in a slightly different way, to show the four sectors which modern economic analysts use to assess employment trends. If this is done the extraordinary switch from manufacturing to services is even more clear:

Sector	1891	1999
Primary	1%	6%
Manufacturing	64%	17%
Construction	5%	6%
Services	31%	72%

This change has been accompanied by a reshaping of the labour force itself. The rise of female employment, just beginning in the late Victorian period, means that today some sectors are staffed mainly by women, but that has been associated with a massive growth in part-time work. Women are still greatly over-represented in lower levels of the employment hierarchy, in part-time and

By the early 20th century white collar workers began to appear in the offices of local firms. Here is a rare portrait of the male-dominated world of the invoice ledger clerk. Even when women eventually joined their ranks it would take at least another 50 years before they could expect equal pay.

By World War One Wood's Tutorial College was offering training courses for 'women and girl clerks' who would be taught by the 'winners of the World's Junior Typewriting Championship Cups of 1910-1912'. The world of the civil servant and the professions also beckoned under their expert instruction.

lower-paid work. Thus, in the crucial service sector, men occupied 62 per cent of full-time posts and only 19 per cent of part-time ones, even though almost 53 per cent of the total workforce in this sector is female. Manufacturing is, not unexpectedly, a male-dominated world – 75 per cent of employees in this sector are men, and among the 25 per cent who are female almost a quarter are in part-time work. When we think about the working lives of Warrington people in the past, today and in the future, issues such as these are of major importance. It might seem a bit too statistical, but that is the best way to demonstrate these far-reaching changes in the life of the town and every one of its people.

These labourers on the Manchester Ship Canal undoubtedly included many Irish workers. At the turn of the 20th century the Irish labourers played an essential role in the workforce but as Harry Hardman recalls they faced a great deal of prejudice from the local population, akin to 21st century hostility towards asylum seekers.

"They used the Irish always to dig the canals, put the roads down and the railways. On the [Manchester] Ship Canal the Irish navvies did the donkey work alright. As a consequence they were herded into the worst properties and they were paid less wages than the English for similar types of work. The Irish were coming into the country, they were bringing a 'foreign' religion with them, Roman Catholicism, and it was mainly Protestants that they were coming amongst. There was that resentment, that hatred. On top of that we had unemployment as we've always had it and they were working for less wages. The bosses were exploiting the Irish more than the English. The Irish had no background as an industrial society. They were agricultural, prepared to work for less than the English lads – so the boss picked the Irish lads didn't he? Prepared to work for less, they worked a damn sight harder to keep their jobs. Healthy, tough fellows – people don't emigrate from any country unless they're tough and healthy, they dare not if they have not got the health to stand up to the conditions they will meet. Of course the Irish lads have always been heavy drinkers. You could always guarantee on a Saturday night a free fight because the English fellows would be waiting to get their own back for taking their jobs, and maybe their women as well. English people, hoodlums I'd call them, would go looking for the Irish lads and the Irish lads would never back down. There would be a free fight, blood and snot and hair would be flying!"

Working Lives and Working Conditions

WE CAN also think about the conditions in which people passed their working lives. Today a good many Warrington people spend the working day in air-conditioned offices, centrally heated in winter, cooled in summer, with large plate-glass windows letting in maximum daylight, or entirely artificial lighting producing a different quality of illumination. Outside there may be areas of grass and trees and a large car park, to which the office workers drive from their homes in other suburbs or out in the countryside of south Lancashire and north Cheshire. The working environment is likely to be clean, smoke-free, dirt-free, and to a very considerable extent hazard-free and danger-free. Of course not everybody works in such conditions but, even in industrial complexes, modern design, health and safety considerations, and planning and building regulations seek to ensure that to an ever-greater extent the workplace is controlled and safe. The likelihood that an employee in Warrington lives in, above, beneath or next to his or her workplace is small, for most people travel to work, often from a considerable distance. Working hours are controlled not only by legislation but also by agreement and contract between worker and employer, paid holidays are guaranteed, statutory holidays and leave are available to all, and the working week is, in principle, shorter than ever before. Here, too, there are many exceptions, but for most employees these benefits are there by right.

How different it was in the past – in many cases, the very recent past – is something which we easily forget. The working lives of Warrington people only 50 years ago were astonishingly different from those of today's citizens, and the lifestyles and opportunities accepted as commonplace now would have seemed impossible dreams in the early 20th century. This is not only a matter of material wealth and spending power, but of the workplace environment and the demands placed upon the labour force. For example, the descriptions of the wireworks, foundries and metalworking shops of the late 19th century, and the photographs which have come down to posterity from that period, demonstrate the alarming

Lying down on the job was not normally encouraged at Houghton's Wireworks or any other Warrington workplace, but this staged photograph gives a rare insight into early 20th century working conditions. Bare white-washed brick walls, a plethora of belts and pulleys, unguarded machinery and worn work benches would have been taken for granted by workers who were unfamiliar with modern concepts of health and safety regulations, paid holidays, sickness benefits and pensions.

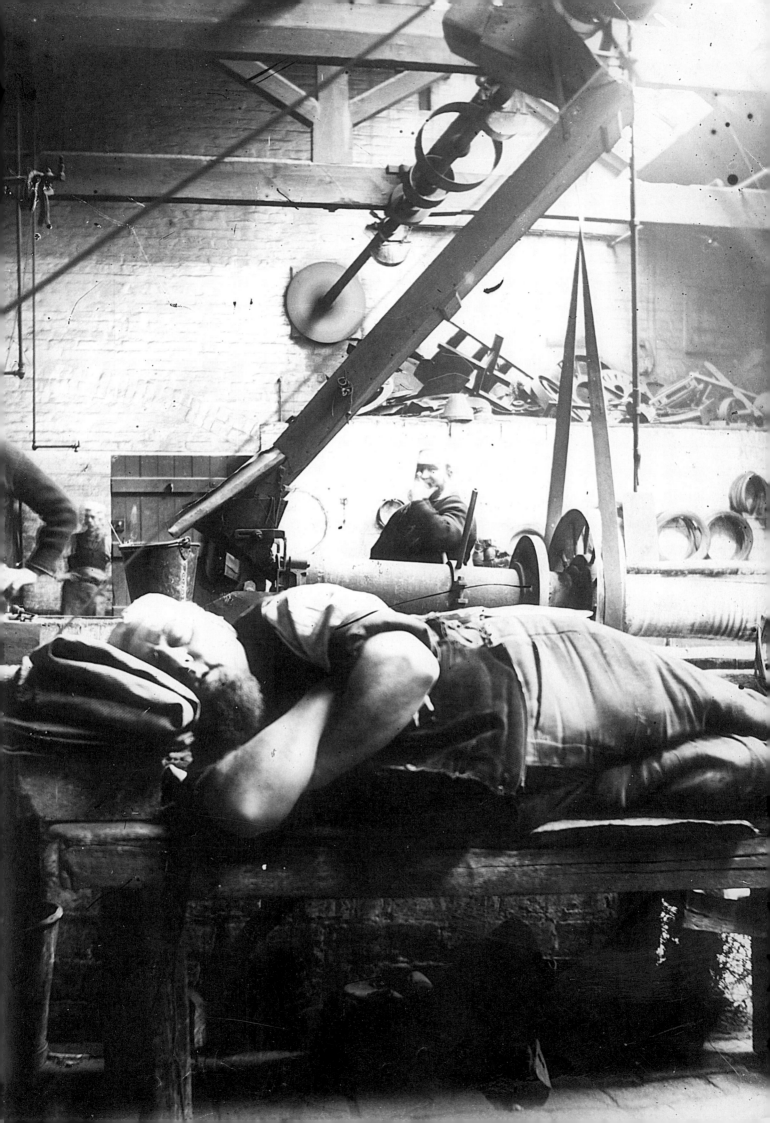

disregard for 'health and safety'. The unguarded machinery, incredibly hard manual labour, high-risk and acutely dangerous production methods, and appalling working conditions are all too evident. Pictures, descriptions and, above all perhaps, the oral testimony bear witness to the dangers of industrial employment. Tannery workers balanced on the edge of pits of corrosive and stinking lime liquid and breathed the harsh and burning dust of the lime powder. Foundry workers laboured just inches from the rivers of white-hot metal whilst filemakers rained blows upon their chisels as they cut the grooves in the face of the tool. The navvies on the Manchester Ship Canal worked with barrows and shovels in unprotected and unshored excavations and children made pins, pinching tiny fragments of wire between large metal blocks. These and many others saw the reality of industrial employment and many suffered accordingly.

Factory buildings and workshops suffered from the extremes of heat and cold, the lack of ventilation or the excess of it, toxic fumes and caustic smoke causing a fetid atmosphere as people, unhealthy and often with infectious diseases, worked cheek-by-jowl. All this contributed to high rates of early death, crippling illness or physical deterioration among the workforce. The social reformers of the mid-Victorian period recorded their disquiet at these circumstances and sought to improve them. Heroic and hard-pressed medical men such as James Kendrick in the 1840s and 1850s worked tirelessly to improve the lot of the workers in Warrington's industries and workshops. Eventually legislation, factory inspection and workplace registration made a real difference to the

The working conditions of these employees of Waring's Tannery would horrify a modern day factory inspector!

working conditions of Warrington people, but it was a slow process and throughout the 20th century gradual improvement continued.

Campaigning for better conditions was sometimes carried on by the trade unions, which started to play a major role in the 1880s. In most family-owned private firms the unions were either forbidden or remained very much in the background, but in some heavy industries, and especially in trades such as textiles, they became important to the well-being of the workforce.

Their value was not especially that they conducted high-profile campaigns, but rather that they provided sickness benefits and financial assistance, and pressed for minor but overdue changes in working practices and matters such as health and safety. Much of the attention, then as now, focussed on the spectacular cases – the factories and the industrial premises – but we should not forget how hard life could be for many other workers. Think of the young shopgirls, who were expected to work 10 and 11 hour days six days a week, doing hard physical labour for small pay: or the self-employed seamstresses and bonnet makers, who bent over their work in dwindling daylight, straining their eyes to thread and sew in the light of gas jets. Think of the farmworkers on the edge of town, ploughing and sowing and reaping and mowing in all weathers and conditions, often without the help of any machinery and sleeping in barns and sheds. Think of the children who, well into the late 19th century, received little or no schooling and were put to work in pinshop or mill or field from the age of seven or eight.

Some employers made genuine efforts to improve the lot of their workforce, and had a strong social conscience which dictated that benefits should be available. They became widely known as good and responsible employers. Perhaps the best known was the Crosfield family whose liberal and enlightened social philosophy was applied in practice: sickness benefits, relatively generous working hours, a wide range of social facilities and leisure activities, and a pervasive air of benevolent paternalism characterised one of Warrington's most prominent, and fastest-growing, industrial concerns. But for most workers such advantages were not available, and working conditions remained less than satisfactory.

The evidence is there for us to see, and as well as being fascinated by it for the historical story which it tells, we should also be aware of how much improvement there has been in our own time. Today most people, to varying degrees, have a choice in what work they do. Of course that does not apply to every citizen of Warrington in the early 21st century, but there is a remarkable amount of freedom and flexibility. We can choose careers, decide on jobs and make decisions about our futures. For a majority of school-leavers higher education in some form is the next step. In the past this was feasible only for a tiny minority

Although the British Aluminium Company were participating in this Health and Safety week in 1956 in reality such precautions were normally ignored. In many workplaces industrial injuries were treated as the norm as David recalls from his days at British Wedge Wire:

"Today they wouldn't let you use the machines we made conveyor belts with. The women actually ran the wire through their hands. They put their foot on a pedal and the wire had a sharp edge and it spun. They ran it through their hands, cut it up, put it down, ran it and cut it. Every now and again you'd hear a woman scream as she put the wire through her fingers. It has gone straight through and out the other side and kept going till they took their foot off the pedal. I cut a few out and just before the factory closed down I did it myself. I looked up and the next thing is that the wire had gone right through my hand. I cut it both sides, got hold of a pair of pliers and pulled it. Next thing I knew the nurse is looking down at me. I'd passed out but I don't remember hitting the floor. It was common and you didn't fill in an accident form or anything like that. I had two hours rest, a hot cup of tea, they bandaged it up and I was back at work because if I went home I lost all my pay."

of the population. Children left school early and went into whatever job they could. Most, indeed, had their futures decided for them by parents or, more often, by circumstances. You went into Rylands because your father, your uncle and your elder brother were already there. You got a position in service in a big house in Palmyra Square because your mother knew someone who gave you a recommendation. You didn't necessarily want to do that, but that was how it was. The idea of going to university, even of studying until you were 18, of 'making good', was exceptional. And the notion that what you did when you were 20 might be nothing like what you would do at 30 or 40 or 50 was never contemplated. Jobs were for life, or as near to life as you could make them. Chopping and changing, career breaks, gap years, retraining ... nobody had heard of such things. Life was in some ways more straightforward but in other ways had less potential, and working conditions were invariably worse. We may grumble and complain about our own working lives and the conditions and circumstances in which we operate, but who would willingly swap with the careworn, weary people, old before their time, who look out at us from so many of those Victorian and Edwardian photographs?

A female employee of Richmond's in the 1920s demonstrates the lack of protective equipment routinely available to workers. However, the firm's medical examinations did identify workers at risk and some might be offered alternative employment.

The 1920s and 30s saw attempts to introduce trade unions into local workplaces but even activists like Harry Hardman found it an uphill struggle. He recalls trying to organise the workforce at Rylands in the 1930s. "The unions were very, very weak. To be in a union, and the firm knowing it, was inviting the sack for the fact that you were in the union. People accept these things now, like holidays with pay, but whether people realise it or not, all the facilities available today, decent working conditions, holidays with pay, pensions, they've all had to be extracted from the employer, and extracted is the right word... People who attempted to organise trade unions had to do it under cover. They wouldn't have trade union representation in the factory. In the 1930s I was collecting for the General Workers Union, trying to recruit men into the union and managed to get a handful. They were afraid of being seen to be in a union, so they used to say: 'Where's your coat?' They'd put their union card and the money in it. This was Rylands as late as 1935-6-7."

By the mid-20th century immigrants from Britain's former colonies were beginning to replace the Irish navvies in Warrington's workforce. The British Aluminium Company included this specially-posed photograph with detailed biographies in their in-house journal in June 1960 to mark the visit of a Mr Reynolds whose company had extensive bauxite interests in Jamaica. On the right is Aubrey Rodney who had emigrated from Spanish Town, St Catherine's in 1954 and was employed as an extrusion press charger; on the left is Egbert Gordon, the youngest of a family of nine from Jamaica, who was a furnace discharger.

A few years later, David recalls working in a wireworks off Mersey Street where Pakistani labourers had been taken on: "It was a very old building, Victorian. There were the first wave of immigrants working there. There were ladies with saris on and on the ground floor in the yard they had a group of Pakistani men. It had an earth floor and they had a great trough full of red lead paint. They dipped screens between them by hand in red lead paint. The charge hand was the only one who spoke good English."

Richmond's pristine medical centre is pictured here in the mid-1920s. Although several Warrington firms introduced such facilities and even a gymnasium at this period, many employees remained sceptical of their effectiveness and also their employers' commitment to workers' welfare.

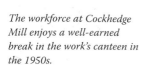

The workforce at Cockhedge Mill enjoys a well-earned break in the work's canteen in the 1950s.

Two members of Monks Hall's Bowling team compare score cards. For many employees their workplace not only dictated their daily grind but the firm's social club filled their leisure time too.

Full steam ahead for employees of Richmond & Co as they head off on a special work excursion to Blackpool early in the 20th century. At a time when paid holidays were still unheard off such an outing might be an employee's only opportunity to take a trip to the seaside.

Crosfield's' Girl Guides make camp at Primrose Valley, Filey, in the late 1920s. Crosfield's were noted as one of the town's more enlightened employers and provided numerous leisure and educational opportunities for their workforce. For many of the teenage girls pictured here this excursion was a great adventure and marked their first holiday away from home. Seventy years later one of the participants could still remember the novelty of discovering a large turtle washed up on the beach and the communal effort of carrying it back to the sea!

Crosfield's Perfection Soap Works Band poses proudly with yet another newly-won trophy. In an effort to keep their workforce out of the pub the teetotal Crosfield family also provided the opportunity to take part in the work's choir or to perform in the firm's specially built theatre.

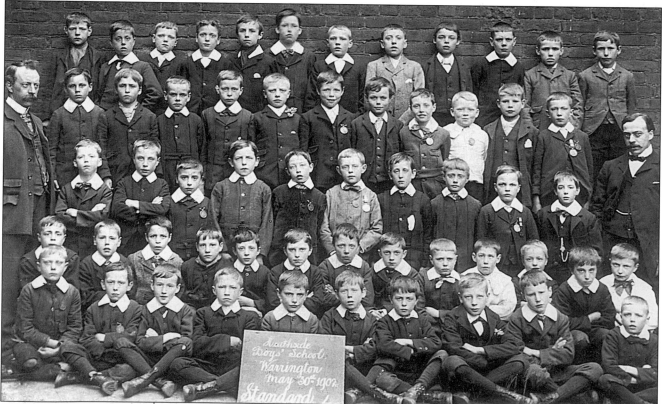

A class from Hamilton Street School poses for the obligatory school photograph but all too soon even the brightest pupil would be thrust into the adult world of work. In the early 20th century, before the introduction of the Welfare State, the concept of a carefree childhood had no place in the life of the poorest families. Everyone had to contribute to the family income, as Harry Hardman recalls:"My brother started work at 13. If your father had been killed in World War One you had the privilege of starting work at 13 because the school leaving age was 14. I can remember the headmaster of Hamilton Street coming to our house at dinnertime and he was praying to our mother to let our Billy go to Grammar School. My mother said: 'There's nothing I'd like better but I can't afford it. I've been waiting and praying for this lad to start work.' She'd been struggling with no fellow behind her. He started at the wireworks making springs and he was good, quick, clever. I don't know what he earned but it altered our standard of living which started to pick up."

The young residents of Padgate Industrial School would have to make their own way in the world without the support of a family so they were taught a trade. Sitting in the traditional cross-legged position of a tailor they learn how to tack a garment together or even how to use a treadle sewing machine. Later they would be apprenticed out to the trade with little say in their future.

Harry Hardman (left) became an active campaigner for the local Labour Party and for the trade union, and above all the rights of the working-classes. He was under no illusions about where the real power lay: "Discipline in the workplace was rigid. The foreman was the sergeant-major for the people above him. The people above him were gentlemen because they kept well away from the reality of work. They left it to the bullying foreman or the managers to crack the whip all the time. The real discipline was unemployment. You were in no position, and nobody else was, to stand up for what you considered the right, because the boss could walk out and pick 10, 20, 30 men standing at the gates."

Young school leavers soon found that real education began in the work place as apprentices. Much depended on their relationship with the older worker who was to train them on the job as David recalls: "One of my friends got an apprenticeship with a man who used him as a dogsbody. He'd give my friend a clip round the earhole and made his life hard but he had to put up with that. There was no point going to the foreman because he wasn't going to listen. You might get a benevolent foreman but you were only making trouble for yourself because you had to go back and work with this man."

Harold Hayes, a young apprentice at the Firth Company, proudly holds up his apprenticeship papers in the early 1920s. Even when a young man had served an apprenticeship there was often no guarantee of a job in the economic depression of the 1930s as Harry Hardman recalls: "I got the sack at Rylands when I was 21. Do you know what the crime was? I was too old at 21. At 21 they paid you £2 2s [£2 10p] a week. That was totally uneconomic. They had to face foreign competition and all sorts, so they gave you the sack and started another lad of 14 on 12 bob (60p) a week."

In times of fuller employment like the 1960s there were usually other jobs to be had, as David explains, "A lot of apprentices were finished up when they were 21 but they had a trade.. They could go to other places and show their certificates and get a job."

Today's workforce is highly-mobile and the concept of a job for life has virtually disappeared. By contrast, in April 1954, the British Aluminium Company held two celebration dinners to acknowledge the contribution of 200 men and women workers who had each given 25 years service to the firm. Naturally everyone received the traditional token of a watch to mark the occasion.

From Field to Table

TODAY we might not associate Warrington with farming and agriculture, but in the past this was an important element of the life of the town. Until the early 20th century there were farms within the boundaries of the old borough, and only with the great expansion of the built-up area from the 1950s was much of the farmland in the vicinity lost to development. The relationship between the town and its rural surroundings was close and mutually beneficial. Warrington provided the services which country people needed – shops and markets, to buy goods unavailable in the villages and (no less vital) to serve as the outlets for farm produce. The rural areas provided much of the food sold and consumed within the town, supplied its milk and cheese and butter, and produced raw materials such as hides and grain which were processed in its breweries, tanneries and flour mills. These patterns, dating back centuries, were eroded and largely destroyed during the 20th century, as mass-produced food, long-distance transport, cheap foreign imports and new marketing methods transformed retailing and people's purchasing habits. The relationship between town and countryside remains close, but for different reasons. The rural areas are valued for leisure and recreation, for landscape and scenery, for ecological and conservation reasons ... and as a highly desirable place to live.

Life on the farm was hard and the popular image beloved of sentimental Victorian painters and poets of a blissful rural tranquillity, of happy country dwellers who lived a wholesome and healthy life, is frequently belied by contemporary accounts. These demonstrate that rural deprivation and poverty was a real problem in the 19th century. In the Warrington area there are several distinct types of soils and landforms, so that agriculture was varied. North of the river, and especially around Woolston, the edge of Chat Moss, Risley and Culcheth, the extensive mosslands were being reclaimed for farming from the 16th century onwards. Typically these improved lands, once drained and fertilised with top-dressing and animal dung, were excellent for intensive market gardening, which grew in importance as the population of south Lancashire increased rapidly in the 18th century. Farmers planted crops such as celery, leeks and cabbage for the Warrington market. Many of these ran smallholdings, on which all the members of the family worked – sowing, weeding, hoeing and harvesting were labour-

By the 1840s Warrington Market Place was a focus for country people trading grain, vegetables and meat at the weekly markets and also livestock at the fortnightly Wednesday fairs. Dairy produce such as farm fresh butter and cheese was also on offer at the temporary trestle tables in front of the Barley Mow Inn.

Local photographer Thomas Birtles captured this idyllic scene of farming life near his Padgate home at the beginning of the 20th century.

intensive tasks, and women and children were expected to give their full share of backbreaking toil.

Dairy-farming was very important from the medieval period onwards. Both north and south of Warrington were major cheese-producing areas – in the early 18th century the white cheese made between Warrington, Leigh, and Prescot was held to be even finer than the best produce of Cheshire. But industrialisation and urban growth began to reduce the farmland in this district and by the end of the 18th century the north Cheshire farms had cornered the market. Then, as Warrington expanded rapidly as an industrial centre, and its population grew accordingly, a new demand for dairy products was generated. Farms in parishes such as Grappenhall, Stockton Heath, Walton, Sankey and Martinscroft responded to the demand by building up the fresh milk trade. A typical sight by the middle of the 19th century – and right through to World War Two – was the horse-drawn or donkey-drawn milk cart, laden with churns, plodding down into the town every day and then doing the rounds of the streets or standing on the market. The same carts often carried butter and maybe some cheese, but the main trade was in milk, sold by the jugful in conditions which would now cause consternation among public health inspectors – dusty, unchilled and unrefrigerated, in cans and churns which were perhaps not properly sterilised, and from cows which might well have infection and be accommodated in far from spotless conditions. Even in the town there were milk-farms, where cows were, not in fields and shippons, but in sheds in backyards. The last of these, Warrington Farm (located, extraordinary though it might seem, in Upper Bank Street just where the market is today) survived until just before World War One. Butchers kept their own herds and flocks: thus Singleton's had a herd of cattle at Appleton, and in the 1930s they had a flock of over 1,500 sheep grazing on the riverside land at Latchford.

For many people on the edge of the town and in the rural parishes beyond, working life was guided and dictated by the cycle of the seasons: ploughing in January and February; sowing in March and April; harvesting in late August and September; turning the animals out to pasture in April; mowing the first hay crop in late June and the second in early September; gleaning in the cornfield after harvest in September; weeding in the fields in May and June; digging potatoes during the late spring or pulling the leeks in the bitter winter when your hands were frozen; or resting briefly under the hedgerow taking a break from the hot, dusty work of harvest ... out in all weathers, not a day passing without something to be done in field or shippon, animals to tend; calving and lambing to supervise; pigs to slaughter and dung to cart. It was never romantic and rarely gentle ... and for the labourers and their families it was poorly-paid and meant hours which would now seem impossibly long. The people on the lowest rung of the farming ladder were the seasonal labourers, especially the Irish who, from the early 18th century onwards, came over for the harvest and the vegetable-picking. These bands of young and not-so-young men, very rarely accompanied by their families, walked from farm to farm across the Warrington area, sleeping in 'paddy shants' – wooden shacks and huts or the lofts of barns and byres – and in most years following the same path so that they went through familiar territory. The object of fear, derision, and pity, but at the same time essential to the working of the farming system, they were a distinctive feature of rural life in the Warrington area until the late 19th century, when mechanisation, the decline of labour-intensive agriculture and a surplus of rural labour put an end to the old tradition.

Food processing industries were significant in Warrington for much of the 19th and 20th centuries. Agricultural produce had hitherto been sold fresh, or converted on the farm into cheese and butter, or in the case of grain was milled to flour locally. After the 1820s, though, larger enterprises began to appear, catering for the mass markets in the hungry industrial towns and cities and making use of improved transport links to deliver foodstuffs further afield. A good example was the flour-milling business founded by James Fairclough at Bank Quay in 1831 and extended by the acquisition of the Mersey Mills at Howley in 1862. The mills were water-powered (the Mersey Mill was claimed to be England's largest watermill) and the river was used for transport – a fleet of

Local farmers relied on seasonal itinerant labourers like this gleaner at Arpley to help with the harvests. Mrs Burke remembers the Irish agricultural labourers in the 1920s. "The Irish workers used to come over in the summer – just from about April until the harvest in September and then they all used to go back home. We used to call them 'Come-overs'. We used to go and watch them in the 'paddy shants'. Those were like little outhouses belonging to the farms. Every farm had a paddy shant. The men used to sleep on straw. I don't think they ever undressed themselves. They used to eat raw bacon and cut a big chunk of bread. The farmers used to give them a lot of potatoes and they used to eat jacket potatoes. That used to amuse us when we were kids. We thought it was funny eating potatoes with the skins on because Dad used to boil them for the pigs with the skins on."

Gartons of Warrington made a great contribution to arable farming by offering new and improved varieties of seeds. Here Dr. John Garton is hard at work cross-fertilising cereal crops at their trial grounds at Acton Grange. Here hybridised varieties of oats, barleys, wheats, grasses, clovers, turnips, mangels and other plants were raised. Much of the advances were a result of John Garton's patient work. A contemporary tribute records: 'His work has resulted in an incalculable increase in the amount of foodstuffs given forth by the earth... not only of British-grown food crops but also of those of foreign countries.' Garton's ceased to operate in 1983, too early to adopt today's controversial techniques of genetically modifying crops.

purpose-built boats brought imported wheat from Liverpool and took the milled flour to warehouses at Widnes and Liverpool for distribution. In the 1950s the firm was taken over by Allied Mills, which included the Sunblest bakery group, and in the late 1970s the Bank Quay mill was still processing 60,000 tons of flour each year. In 1984, though, the closure of Scott's bakery in Liverpool removed the main market for Warrington flour and the mill at Bank Quay closed. A similar fate had already befallen the Mersey Mills, taken over in 1948 by what became North West Farmers and converted to the production of almost 2,000 tons of animal feedstuffs per week. Changing technology and a decision to concentrate production on another plant were blamed when the mills closed in September 1970 with the loss of 90 jobs. Gaskell Brothers, the bacon-curers of Woolston, had facilities for the slaughter of 5,000 pigs per week, but that did not prevent a financial crisis which led to abrupt closure in June 1986, with 130 redundancies. Businesses such as these had been a logical development from earlier industries which made use of the output of local agriculture. When they were established in the heyday of 19th-century economic expansion, they were 'state of the art' concerns, and most – such as Faircloughs and North West Farmers, invested heavily in the 1930s and 1950s to bring plant and equipment up to date. But by the 1970s radical restructuring in the industry, fast-changing technology, shifting patterns of demand from the consumer, and – in the case of the bakery and flour industry – problems with industrial relations, meant that the plants were no longer seen as viable. They closed, and by 1990 there was little left of Warrington's once important food processing industries.

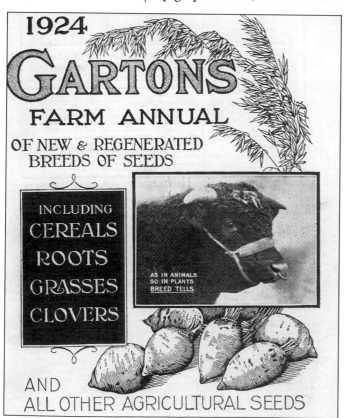

1924

GARTONS
FARM ANNUAL
OF NEW & REGENERATED BREEDS OF SEEDS

INCLUDING
CEREALS
ROOTS
GRASSES
CLOVERS

AS IN ANIMALS
SO IN PLANTS
BREED TELLS.

AND
ALL OTHER AGRICULTURAL SEEDS

In the early 20th centuries the milk cart was an everyday sight in most Warrington streets. Unpasteurised milk from local farms was ladled out from a churn into unsterilised jugs brought out by the customers. Advances in hygiene led to the development of highly-organised dairies like Rigby's Mill Bank Dairy at Grappenhall, opened in 1948. Milk-lorries brought their cargo from outlying dairy farms to this central plant where the milk was cleaned and sterilised by the pasteurisation process and then transferred to sterilised glass bottles for delivery.

The ploughman plods his weary way at Brook House Farm Penketh in 1902.

Ploughing at Padgate in the early 1900s before the tractor replaced horse-power and the traditional field boundaries were ripped out to provide access to the modern machinery.

This haymaking scene near Quarry Lane at Appleton had hardly changed for centuries when it was recorded in the early 1900s.

By World War One progressive farmers were moving away from the traditional labour-intensive methods. Contractors could be hired in at harvest time bringing the power of their steam engine to drive a mighty threshing machine.

The farm horse waits patiently with his load of hay, apparently undisturbed by the monstrous machinery beside him. The occasion was still enough of a novelty for a local amateur photographer to record the new machinery.

Even as late as the 1960s there were still pockets of farm land in inner Warrington. This harvesting scene took place in the middle of the Loushers Lane housing estate and under the shadow of the Cantilever Bridge over the Manchester Ship Canal.

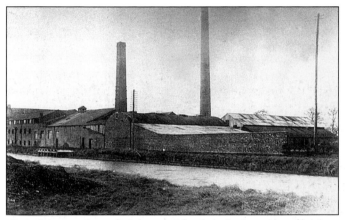

Gorton's boneworks marked the end of the chain for the residue of local livestock but for nearby residents at Paddington it was notorious for the noxious smells which emitted from the works.

Livestock farming was still big business in the days before qualms over BSE and increased interest in vegetarianism. The unrefrigerated display outside Singleton's Bridge Street Shop may look unhygienic but, as the Royal warrant above the shop sign reveals, they were deemed worthy to supply to Queen Victoria.

Sir Gilbert Greenall of Walton Hall specialised in livestock breeding and his herd of pedigree Large Whites was world famous. John Neaverson, the head pig man, is pictured here with one of his prize-winning sows. A careful food regime was necessary to ensure success but as he explained: "We do not produce fat pigs of any description except for show. There is a large export trade for both boars and gilts, and our pigs will be found as foundation stock in every part of the world."

Mr Joseph Shaw, seen here in 1905, was one of Warrington's oldest established butchers. Many firms were concentrated around the old Market area as a reminder of the days when cattle had been driven to Warrington Market on the hoof and slaughtered behind the butcher's premises.

Fairclough's extensive mills were served by their own specially-built barges, Panary *and* Pater*, which could navigate speedily to Warrington with their cargoes of grain.*

Leather and Tanning

AD you walked down Mersey Street in, say, the hot summer of 1870, you might have been all too aware of a pervasive stench emanating from some of the buildings round about – though if you were a resident of central Warrington you had probably long been used to the smell. Perhaps a stroll down Tanners Lane and through the closely-packed areas of poor housing on the northern edge of the old town would have made you aware of a similar odour. Among the traffic clattering down the street there might have been horse-drawn wagons laden with great piles of animal skins, already 'high' and still with scraps of meat, layers of fat, and greening flesh adhering to the inner side. Peering through the gates and archways into which these wagons turned you might have seen more heaps of skins, or perhaps a series of long rectangular pits filled with noxious liquid, from which men with long hooked poles were picking dripping, slimy skins. These were the tanneries, for generations one of Warrington's most important (and, to many people, least pleasant) industries, and the mainstay of its flourishing trade in leather goods.

Tanning and leather-working had been Warrington trades since the Middle

A 1930s aerial view of Waring's Tannery which covered a four acre site between Winwick Street and Dallam Lane. At this time the tanning industry was still a major employer in the town, with tanneries concentrated around Winwick Road, Mersey Street, Howley, Latchford, Penketh and Orford.

This
Flem
Stree
tann
back
patt
whic
of ch
untr
hide
are
with
wine
hide
arou
sma
who
ofte
stem

The tanning process began with
the arrival of dry hides which had
been imported from all over the
world and probably unloaded at
Bishop's Wharf for the final leg of
their journey by road.

waters which flowed down from Manchester were made much more noxious by the time they reached Fiddlers Ferry and had received the outflow of tannery waste. In the 19th century, as the town grew around the older tannery sites, there were repeated concerns over the pollution of drinking water supplies as well as frequent complaints over the smells which emanated from the works.

Tannery work was arduous, poorly-paid and dangerous. Death by drowning was far from rare, as men fell into the deep and corrosive waters of the pits. As awareness of public health and hygiene grew in the 20th century the risk of infection from handling the hides became apparent. Jack Hamlett, works manager at Howley Tanneries from 1934, recalled how the danger of contracting anthrax was a particular fear, and any worker with a spot or boil was whisked off to the specialist unit at Fazakerley Hospital to be tested. Back in the 19th century such measures were unknown, and tanning was a filthy and hazardous trade. Men wore great leather aprons and heaved vast dripping hides in and out of pits, balancing on the narrow walkways. There were women workers too, mainly at the 'leather end' of the production process, where the tanned hides were polished and burnished and cut to size ready to be made up.

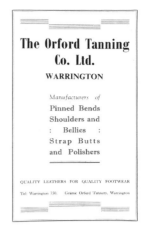

Tannery labour was back-breaking and hazardous because of the chemicals involved. The workers' only protective clothing was a sturdy waterproof linen 'brat' or apron, leather or waterproof leggings and clogs which gave a better grip on the slimy wooden floors than rubber soles.

Leather supported a range of other trades. Warrington never became a great centre for the footwear industry (unlike, for example, Nantwich) but it had several large clogmakers and the town's tanneries supplied the leather for clog soles. They also produced the leather soles for military and police boots, heavy duty, thick and hard-wearing, and in the early 20th century Warrington was England's main supplier. Another product in which the town's leather producers

Products from Warrington's tanneries also found their way into local cobblers' shops. Here inmates of Padgate Industrial School are tutored in the craft of bootmaking.

By the 1930s Whittle & Sons patent leather belting was exported all over the world for driving train lighting, dynamos, coalmining machinery, wood working machinery, pumps, fans, cotton, paper, tanning and grinding machinery, motor cars, machine tools and all kinds of electric motors. Perhaps because of this diversity of clients they were able to survive the foreign competition which led to the demise of most of Warrington's other tanneries by the late 20th century.

"WHITTLE" Patent
(Regd. Trade Mark)
BELTING

Combines Strength, Flexibility, Perfect Grip and SILENCE.

THE IDEAL DRIVE FOR LINE SHAFTS AND SHORT CENTRE DRIVES.

Drives arranged to suit any centres. No slide rails or tensioning device. Easily fitted between bearings. No fasteners.

T. WHITTLE & SONS, LTD.

Telephone—**365**　WARRINGTON　Telegrams –"BELT,"
Warrington　　　　　　　　　　　Warrington

Brewing

THERE were many parallels between the leather trade and brewing, one of the other mainstays of the town's later industrial base. Both used the products of local agriculture, both were ancient trades established in Warrington many generations before their expansion in the late 18th century, both showed the split between old sites close to the centre and newer greenfield locations on the edge of the town, and both suffered as a result of the changing commercial world of the later 20th century. Brewing is one of the oldest trades and was well-nigh universal. By the Middle Ages every town had brewers operating on a commercial scale (though output was minute by later standards). In Warrington, as elsewhere, the activities of public brewers concerned the authorities. First, brewers (who usually sold beer on their premises as well) contributed to the scourge of drunkenness and rowdy behaviour, and second, like

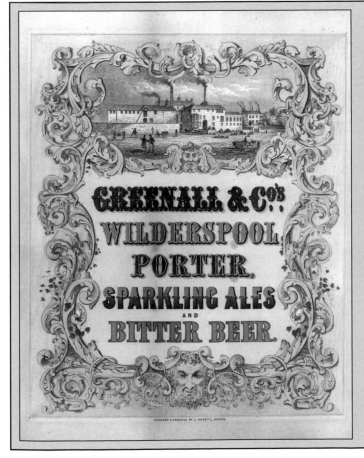

Greenall's Wilderspool Ales originated from the old Saracen's Head brewery and maltings, seen here in this early trade advertisement. Successive generations of the family were actively engaged in the business, moving from the White House – founder Thomas Greenall's home (seen on the extreme right) – to a country estate at Walton Hall. As the business prospered the brewing dynasty became leading political figures in the town. Their Conservative views made them more resistant to the introduction of the trade union into their operations, as a former employee recalls: "I had a full family of uncles and aunties who all worked at Greenalls. We had to charge 1s 6d a week for our union, 1s 0d went to the union itself and sixpence was a levy. Because people were Conservative they wouldn't pay the levy. We were trying to introduce the Transport and General Workers' Union but Greenalls didn't want the union. They were all Conservatives. The majority of people who worked in Greenalls in my day were all in tied houses. When I was hauled over the coals over the union, the house was dangled in front of me. They said I'd have to be careful but I still didn't buckle down. My father was always a very strong union man even though he worked at the same firm. He wouldn't say anything but I did!

"We brought the head man from Manchester and he went to see the head brewer, Mr Ferguson, who was our boss. This man said: 'Look, why shouldn't these men be in a union? You're in a union, the brewers' union.' That's how it started. He fought for us but it was a big struggle... When Tetley's Brewery had a rise we only got the same rise six months afterwards. Tetley's were a big union firm. We thought why should we have to wait six months after Tetley's? We got the union at the end but it was a big struggle."

By the early 1900s the Wilderspool Brewery had been completely rebuilt and housed the most modern equipment, an extensive hop stores, a new bottling stores and cooperageworks, yards and offices, whilst the firm owned a number of licensed houses in Lancashire, Cheshire, North Wales, Shropshire, Staffordshire and other areas as well as the majority of the hotels and inns in Warrington. This aerial photograph of 1900 was taken from a hot air balloon and used as the basis for an early advertising poster.

any other traders, they were not averse to selling substandard products such as watery beer made of unwholesome materials. Alehouses and beerhouses were places where disorder was rife, so the authorities sought to regulate and license them – owners had to make an annual payment for such a privilege. The town's first known byelaws, passed in 1617, included several clauses seeking to control brewing and beerselling.

By the middle of the 18th century brewing was beginning to develop on a larger scale. The real boost came in the 1780s when Thomas Greenall, a small-time brewer from the fast-growing industrial town of St Helens, went into commercial partnership with William Orrett, the Warrington postmaster who was also a merchant, and Thomas Lyon of Appleton Hall, a merchant and industrialist. These men provided the business opportunities and commercial contacts, while Greenall offered expertise, dynamic entrepreneurship, and ambition. They bought the Saracen's Head brewery at Wilderspool, dating from the 1740s, and expanded output so that by 1791 it had to be entirely rebuilt on a much grander scale. From this, the vast Greenall's empire grew. In 1824 Thomas Greenall's son, Edward, took as his financial partner a Liverpool lawyer and solicitor, John Whitley. He not only invested heavily – and profitably – in the business, but also gave it the other half of the name familiar for eight generations.

Why did Warrington become a centre of the British brewing industry? There are all sorts of possibilities. There was a fine supply of pure water from wells at Wilderspool and near the town centre. Locally grown grain had long been converted into malt – one of the 1617 byelaws ordered that malt should only be made at the lord of the manor's mill beside the river at Howley. There was a tradition of brewing – even the famous Peter Stubs, founder of Warrington's great filemaking firm, began his business life as a brewer and publican. But many other towns had comparable advantages so the answer is unclear. What is certain is that the excellence of Warrington's geographical location played an important part in the expansion of the trade. As raw materials were brought from further afield and the output of the brewery was distributed more widely, the efficient transport network of which the town was the focus was a major advantage. Equally, much was down to one man, Thomas Greenall, and his personal decision to go to Warrington to expand his developing brewing concern. Had he chosen to go, say, to Wigan, it is probable that the great brewery would never have been built and brewing would have remained a relatively minor element in Warrington's industrial base.

Greenall's were of course not alone in Warrington, though at times their commercial might and highly-effective publicity machine eclipsed all rivals. The family, who eventually moved out to the rural delights of Walton Hall, maintained their very close links with the town, seeking with considerable skill to rule the roost, dominate the political life of the borough, promote their strong Conservative and conservative values, and outdo their competitors including the Crosfield family, who were equally strongly Liberal and liberal. Other brewers

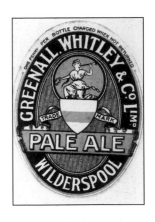

Greenall's fleet of steam lorries stand ready to supply the brewery's tied houses and quench the thirst of working men at the end of their long shifts in Warrington's factories and foundries.

Greenall's had not only embraced the latest technology in the Wilderspool brewery and exploited the new medium of advertising but, as lorry number 18 shows, their clients could also reach them on the new telephone network.

sought to make their mark. In 1864 Peter Walker took over an existing brewery in King Street and two years later opened his Dallam Lane brewery, the second largest in the town. Walker's was a fierce competitor to Greenall's, and tried to emulate the larger firm down the road by using persuasive and progressive marketing techniques. Both companies were pioneers of the 'tied house', and Greenall's eventually became the market leaders – in 1900, with over 1000 houses, they had the largest pub chain in the country. But Walker's chosen image of 'wholesome' public houses was powerful and clever, because it implied that Greenall's tended towards the spit and sawdust end.

As with many other industries, brewing gave rise to a host of other trades on which it depended and which relied on it for their survival. Until the advent of huge automated breweries with slick modern technology, in the years after World War Two, even Greenall's still made use of, for example, specialised craftsmen like the coopers, who manufactured barrels. Peter Walker had a separate coopering department devoted entirely to this business. The same firm also demonstrated what economists call 'vertical integration' – the ownership of different stages in the production process – by acquiring a 50-acre hop farm at Westhope in Herefordshire, supplying most of the company's requirements and allowing it to claim with all truthfulness that it had full control of the quality of its products and raw materials. In 1937, 500 pickers worked for all the month of September to harvest the hop crop.

For brewery workers in the 19th century life was tough. Old-fashioned breweries were labour-intensive and conditions often very difficult. The buildings were intensely hot, because the brew was made in great coppers or vats heated by coal-fired furnaces. As a result, the brewing halls had open louvred windows or vents, which allowed steam to escape and gave a through current of air – that inevitably meant that they were draughty (you couldn't win!) and in the winter months workers would be overheated and chilled simultaneously. In smaller breweries the boiling vats were stirred by hand using great paddles, and the scalding liquid was let off to run along open channels so it cooled as fast as possible. The spent mash, like the malted grain, the sugar and the hops, had to be shovelled by hand. Larger breweries were more mechanised, although the principles on which they operated remained identical, and it was not until the 'high-tech' factories of the later 20th century, with their huge stainless steel vats, miles of piping, efficient coolers and electrical and gas power, that the hard labour disappeared. Bottling and casking involved strenuous manual work, as anyone who has delivered beer casks even today can testify: brewery labourers, loading barrels, crating bottles and shifting mountains of coke and coal, certainly earned their far from princely pay.

The landlord of the Pelican Inn puts out the welcome mat for customers to his Buttermarket Street hostelry. Typical of the elaborate pub architecture favoured by Greenalls in the early 1900s it was embellished with an ornate inn sign and Art Nouveau glazed tiles. The etched windows are emblazoned with the company logos showing a clear appreciation of the value of brand awareness.

In the second half of the 20th century brewing underwent change on a dramatic scale. Nationally there was an inexorable reduction in the number of independent brewers, as smaller companies were gobbled up by larger competitors and – usually – closed down. The industry became exceptionally aggressive in its marketing, and well-known names disappeared. In 1960 Walker's merged with Tetleys, to become Tetley Walker: the firm rebuilt its Dallam Lane brewery in 1967, and the future seemed assured, but its subsequent merger with the European giant Carlsberg not only meant the end of the Walker name but also foreshadowed the closure of the Warrington brewery in 1996.

At the same time, the brewery giants began to buy their way into only loosely related areas such as hotels and restaurants, leisure facilities and entertainment. The result was that their brewing businesses became merely part of much larger

Greenalls had a number of competitors of whom the most prominent were Walker & Son who took over the existing King Street Brewery in 1846 before setting up headquarters in Dallam Lane to sell their Walker's Warrington Ales.

Arms folded, these Walker's workers take a brief rest from their labours to pose at the Dallam Lane brewery early in the 20th century.

conglomerates, whose ramifications, under brand names and hidden ownership, stretched seemingly endlessly away from the original core business. The inevitable next step was that that brewing was regarded as irrelevant and was dispensed with. Modern business methods and the power of vast sums of money left little place for sentiment. In 1991 Greenall's ended the brewing of beer at Wilderspool after a continuous history of almost 250 years, and in 1999 they disposed of all their public houses and restaurants to their rivals, Scottish and Newcastle (itself the product of comparable mergers, takeovers and expansionism). While the Greenall's name just about survives, the firm itself is no more and one of Warrington's most celebrated industries is part of history. In only five years the two great names, Greenall and Walker, disappeared.

By 1990 only a handful of truly independent brewery companies survived, among them Burtonwood Ales, which continues to prosper. It was founded in 1867 by James and Jane Forshaw and at first sold just 20 barrels of ale a week, though the founders followed a far-sighted policy of purchasing public houses to give a guaranteed market. By 1907 Burtonwood was selling over 500 barrels a

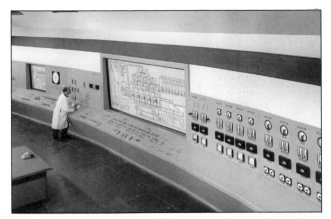

week and had cornered the market in working men's clubs in areas such as Haydock, St Helens and Warrington itself. After 1945, when it had acquired a total of 285 tied houses, the firm was a substantial enterprise, but it retained not only its strong regional base – today it has almost 450 houses, concentrated in south Lancashire, Cheshire, north-east Wales and the north Midlands – but also its strong ties with the Forshaw family. In 2002 its operating profit rose by 7.3 per cent to £9.4 million. Alone among the great names of Warrington brewing, Burtonwood survives.

In 1967 Tetley Walkers embraced the newest technology to introduce a control room which had echoes of the contemporary space programme. Here is the 59 foot illuminated panel which was the control centre of the brewhouse. On the far left is the mimic diagram which covered the intake and blending of malt, whilst the larger diagram covered the brewing process up to the fermentation stage. It was all very scientific, but to many beer lovers such innovations were a world away from 'real ale'.

In the 1970s Greenall's quirky advertisements for their brand of Vladivar vodka almost caused an international incident when the Soviet government failed to see the funny side of a commercial which featured a Communist revolutionary poster of heroic Lenin. The poster was dropped, but the campaign continued and in December 1977 Warrington's good citizens were somewhat alarmed to discover that the Russians appeared to have retaliated by invading Market Gate! A 60 foot mural by popular cartoonist Bill Tidy depicted scenes of Moscow's Red Square with Soviet soldiers dancing with Lancashire girls who were handing out black puddings under the slogan of 'Warrington: The Home of Vladivar Vodka!'

Beer was traditionally supplied to the pubs in wooden casks – often made by the breweries' own coopers. Traditionally the heavy oak barrels were made by time-served craftsmen and represented a costly investment for the breweries. Initially Walkers had bought in over £40,000-worth of casks annually, but as a cost-saving measure invested in electrical machinery to produce all the wooden sections. First the wooden stave was cut to length, then shaped according to the size of the cask, and next it passed through a machine which rounded and hollowed the sections. Finally the skilled coopers took over the operation as the Warrington Guardian describes: "The dressed staves are placed in an iron hoop by the cooper, and put under the steaming cone to make the staves pliable for bending. From the steaming cone the cask passes to the trussing machine where it is bent to the required shape. The cask, being completely trussed, goes to the firing shed where it is placed over a slow wood fire. The staves become set to their new bent position and the moisture imparted to the staves by the steaming process is dried out. The interior of the cask finishes a golden brown, and as this surface comes in direct contact with the beer, it will readily be seen why so many connoisseurs demand 'draught' beer. The cask is now taken by the skilled cooper who makes the chime and groove, afterwards fitting in the heads. No nails are used, yet the cask is to stand 30 pounds pressure,. The heads and staves are held in position by iron hoops."

Tools, Files and Clocks

MOST of the occupations which we have looked at so far have been associated with agriculture. In contrast, the 18th century saw a new range of industries which began as small-scale enterprises, based in cottages and small workshops, but which eventually grew to much larger concerns. Many were connected with metal-working, which by 1850 was the most important element in the economy of Warrington and adjacent parishes on both sides of the river, as well as being of major significance to a wide area from Prescot, through Ashton in Makerfield to Atherton. In this district, since the late 17th century, craftsmen had concentrated on the production of small specialised metal goods. An ordinary blacksmith could readily turn out a 'no frills' piece of agricultural equipment and produce unsophisticated pieces of ironware for domestic, agricultural or industrial use, but there was now a growing demand for items such as chain links, nails, locks and bolts, files, and watch and clock parts,

Tucked away in one of Warrington's nondescript back alleys is what remains of a hand file cutter's workshop.

which were more complex and time-consuming to produce and required highly-skilled craftsmen. These goods were small – sometimes, as with tiny watch springs, exceptionally so – so it was possible for them to be produced in domestic premises with backyard forges.

The more general expansion of industry across the region generated new demands for such items, while the growing market for consumer goods such as watches and clocks also contributed to increasing output in the metal-working trades. Industrialisation required new sorts of tools and equipment, such as files, screwdrivers, technical instruments, fine metal chains, and small parts for engines and machinery. In Warrington and villages such as Grappenhall and Stockton Heath the effect of these developments was soon felt. New ingredients were added to the atmosphere of Warrington – the clink and clash of hammers and wheeze of bellows, the smell and smoke of little coal-fired furnaces, the fumes and heat of annealing and hardening processes, and the rasp and screech of grinding and smoothing and

polishing on sandstone wheels. Such scenes and sounds could be repeated in villages and small towns across south Lancashire, but in Warrington's case the industry eventually acquired a worldwide market and an internationally-renowned name.

That it did so here, rather than in, say, Tyldesley, was largely due to one man, Peter Stubs. He was born in Warrington in 1756 and tradition states that when he was in his late teens he became a filemaker. However, like many others he sought a supplementary source of income – typically, metal-workers might have smallholdings or, elsewhere in the region, might be part-time colliers. Peter Stubs chose to enter the licensed trade and at the end of the 1770s acquired the lease of the White Bear in Bridge Street. For over 20 years he ran the pub and continued to make files in a small workshop behind the inn, but in 1802 he gave up the lease and opened a new fileworks in Scotland Road. This move resulted in a gradual switch from domestic working to the factory system in the town, though well into the 20th century there was still a good deal of cottage production – but whereas in other places the small craftsmen were self-employed, here they were outworkers for the Stubs company.

Stubs died in 1806 but the firm prospered and soon not only dominated the Warrington industry but also became a world leader, capturing the largest share of the fast-expanding market for files and other tools in England and selling very widely overseas. With its greater scale of production and also ability to innovate and respond to new market demands, Peter Stubs' began to manufacture an ever-wider range – thus, as the Prescot watchmaking trade reached its peak in the

This view of Bridge Street looking towards Friars Gate in the late 19th century was the unlikely site for the beginnings of one of Warrington's cutting-edge industries when Peter Stubs began his filemaking enterprise here a century earlier.

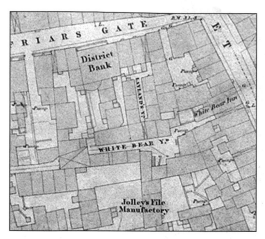

This early Ordnance Survey map shows the location of the White Bear Inn near to the junction of Friars Gate and Bridge Street. Here new landlord Peter Stubs continued his existing trade as a file manufacturer. This combination of occupations perhaps contributed to the superior qualities of Stubs files which were known for their durability and strengths – Stubs' workers used a paste made from the dregs of the inn's beer barrels in the hardening process.

middle years of the 19th century, it was the Scotland Road works which made the tiny files needed to finish the almost invisibly small springs, coils and plates. The works diversified into dental equipment, medical instruments, pliers and nippers, vices and shears. A catalogue produced in the early 1950s by Fred Wright of Latchford, who worked for Stubs for over 40 years, included dozens of highly individual files and other items, each one designed for an specific purpose, each produced for small individual orders, and each identifiable from memory by any skilled craftsman. With names such as 'hand file bastard', 'shoemakers rasp punched square end' and 'slim square needle file 72 cuts/inch safe side' the list speaks about a world of craftsmen with a powerful sense of pride in their job, in which mass production and standardisation had not yet eliminated the extraordinary rich variety of the old ways.

Filemaking was long and complex – a 19th century description referred to 18 consecutive stages by which steel rods were cut, made into blanks, chiselled with tiny grooves, cross-cut, re-cut, cleaned, hardened, finished, polished and coated. It was delicate and yet physically demanding. Workers breathed fine metal dust from grinding, cutting and polishing, and there were many injuries from hammering, burns, flying splinters and cuts. The final stages of cleaning were undertaken by women who sat scouring the files with coconut husks dipped in ashes, before rubbing them down with oil, and wrapping them in paper. Different workers did different stages: the initial cutting and cross-cutting was the responsibility of one man while another would do the hardening stage, which required special skill to avoid spoiling the newly-cut grooves. In the 1940s a retired Stubs employee recalled that a hardener might deal with 48 dozen files a day, about 170,000 a year.

This plan of Stubs' Scotland Road works in 1902 shows the highly-organised nature of the operation by then with departments including the steel warehouse, several forging and cutting shops, the annealing shop, cleaning shop, hardening shop as well as warehouses and offices.

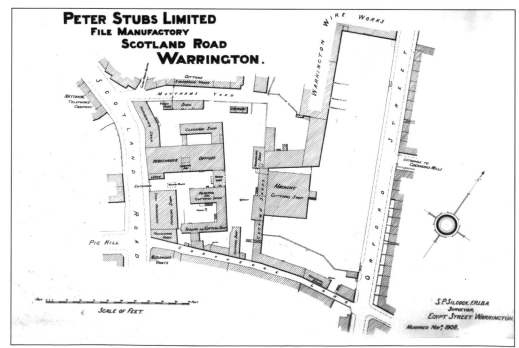

The pay was notoriously bad. Filemakers were among the worst paid workers in the town, despite their skills. Apprenticeships lasted for seven years but wages were often less than those of unskilled labourers – a respected worker with years of experience and a high output might only receive £1 a week in the mid-1870s. The company produced the steel blanks and the employees, working in their cottages, even had to buy from the firm the chisels with which they cut the grooves. In 1891 the industry employed over 400 people in the town but it was not yet mechanised. Only in 1896 was a practical

wheel-cutting machine invented – and even this was manually-operated, and could only work on the coarser and larger files. It was not until the late 1930s that mechanised manufacture became more general, so this industry remained one of the last bastions of the traditional craftsmen and their procedures. They were, of course, destined to disappear. In 1973 the Scotland Road works closed, after 170 years, and Stubs moved to purpose-built modern premises at Wilderspool

Although Stubs concentrated his outworkers into a central operation at Scotland Road, file cutting was still done by hand until the mid-1930s. Interviewed by the Warrington Guardian in 1973 George Strettle recalled his seven years' apprenticeship there and his experiences with the firm from 1925. When he came out of his apprenticeship he was earning between £2 and £2 10s a week and he had real pride in his job, which involved producing files varying in length from 1½ inches to 30 inches. On average he made 32 cuts per inch, working with a hammer and chisel at a pace which could reach 180 cuts an inch, without even having to glance down at his work. "In those days there was a real sense of craftsmanship. Apart from the factory workers there were many 'country hands' making files by hand in the Warrington area. They would come in on Wednesday, all dressed up, and draw a week's pay after handing over a matchbox filled with tiny handmade files.".

Part of the Scotland Road works which produced precision tools, including watch hammers which the firm supplied to clockmakers. Their files were highly-prized in Europe and especially in America, where clockmakers asked specifically for Stubs' files. When America placed a bar on the import of British goods in the early 1800s Stubs found a way of virtually smuggling them into America to avoid the loss of this lucrative market! The fact that Stubs was prepared to give the clockmakers extended credit also helped to build up his client base.

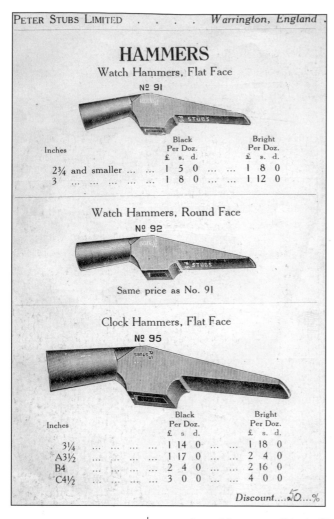

PETER STUBS LIMITED . . . . Warrington, England .

HAMMERS

Watch Hammers, Flat Face
No 91

Inches	Black Per Doz. £ s. d.	Bright Per Doz. £ s. d.
2¾ and smaller	1 5 0	1 8 0
3	1 8 0	1 12 0

Watch Hammers, Round Face
No 92

Same price as No. 91

Clock Hammers, Flat Face
No 95

Inches	Black Per Doz. £ s. d.	Bright Per Doz. £ s. d.
3¼	1 14 0	1 18 0
A3½	1 17 0	2 4 0
B4	2 4 0	2 16 0
C4½	3 0 0	4 0 0

Discount....50....%

*By the mid-1930s Stubs'
switched the whole of their
operation to machine
cutting, also employing
women on the work
benches.*

Causeway. Today, the incredibly rapid and astonishingly accurate blows of hammer on chisel, the rasping of polishing and the hiss of red-hot steel in cold water are a distant memory, and the 1970s concrete of relief roads and office blocks has obliterated almost all trace of the site of this fascinating industry.

Clock- and watchmaking was closely associated with the hand tool trade. Although Warrington was never as important in this as Prescot, the acknowledged local centre, there were several leading makers in the town in the late 18th and early 19th centuries. The presence of Peter Stubs and his toolmaking business undoubtedly helped (Stubs was the main supplier of specialised tools to the American clock industry as well). Warrington's most celebrated watchmaker was James Carter (1780-1848), who was born in the Liverpool area and later moved to live in Buttermarket Street. His business was very successful – all eight of his sons trained as watchmakers as well – and characteristically it was closely integrated with other family concerns. His mother, Margaret Birchall, was a member of a Warrington and Whiston watchmaking family, and his wife, Margaret Simcock of Prescot, was from a family which specialised in movementmaking for the Prescot and Warrington watchmakers. It is indicative of a close-knit and very specialised world, in which different places and families each had their role in the overall business. The Warrington clock and watch makers had other connections – for example, their

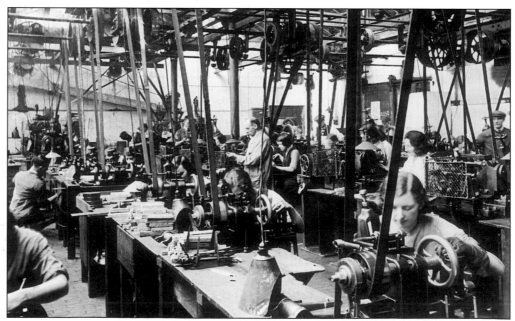

demand for brass to make bells, hammers, pinion wires, dials and clockface decorations was partly responsible for the 18th century brass-founding industry at Bank Quay, while their national and international trade dealings gave Warrington a very wide market and helped to advertise the town and its industries.

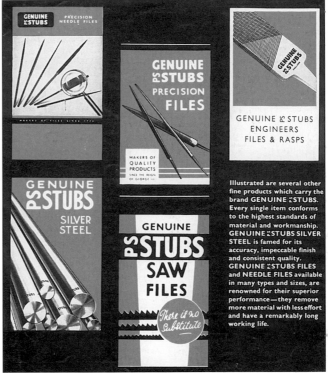

Despite Stubs' dominance of the market there were several other smaller-scale firms supplying the market for specialised tools including Thewlis, Griffith & Edelsten's, Jolley's, Holden's and George Plumpton & Co.

Harry Hill, clock repairer and cabinetmaker, illustrates the close relationship which existed between the two trades.

The Textile Trades

WARRINGTON is not usually thought of as a town with a significant textile industry. Most books about Lancashire cotton ignore it completely, or merely make a passing reference, and even in the town itself it is perhaps not realised how important the cotton industry was. Today hardly a trace remains even of the great cotton mill at Cockhedge – apart, that is, from the girders which were re-used as a token of historical continuity in the construction of the shopping centre now occupying the site. Yet cotton had a long history in Warrington, Cockhedge Mill was large even by Lancashire standards, and some aspects of the textile trade, such as fustian-cutting, were highly distinctive.

A few figures help to put the cotton industry in perspective. In 1921, the year at which the industry was at its peak in Lancashire and Cheshire, 2,163 people in Warrington worked in textiles. This constituted 6.1 per cent of the employed population, but since 90 per cent of those workers were women the industry accounted for 19.9 per cent of female employment in the town. Clearly it was not insignificant, and was very important in providing work for women. But if we set

A view of Armitage & Rigby's Spinning Mill at Cockhedge as seen from the roof of the weaving department.

these figures against those for the somewhat smaller borough of Nelson in east Lancashire a dramatic contrast emerges. In Nelson an extraordinary 68.3 per cent of the entire workforce in the town was employed in the cotton industry, and 81.6 per cent of all jobs for women were in that sector. So although there was cotton at Warrington, and it was important to the town's economy, it was not remotely as dominant as in the east Lancashire towns. Warrington was an outpost of Lancashire's cotton district, geographically and economically. It was all to the good that this was so, for when cotton collapsed in the mid-1920s towns such as Nelson became desperately depressed and have never recovered from that economic catastrophe. Warrington, in contrast, could weather most economic storms because it was not reliant on one vulnerable trade.

Cotton came to Warrington early on in its great period of expansion in the north-west. Peel's cotton works at Latchford, opened in 1787, was one of the earliest large mills in the region and among the first to be steam-powered. A large number of smaller ventures followed, but the industry was precarious. During the trade crisis of 1826-27 there was civil unrest and rioting among the workforce and in 1829 Cockhedge Mills failed in a disastrous financial crash. It reopened two years later, and in the mid-1830s there were 24 mills in the town, most of them very small by Lancashire standards. At the 1841 census over 1,600 cotton workers were listed, so that this was actually the town's largest single employer, but that status was short-lived and from the 1850s most smaller mills went out of

Ethel Whitfield was chosen to take visiting groups around the Mill and so gained a rare experience of the role of departments other than the weaving shed where she normally worked. She recalled: "The raw cotton came as bales to the cotton shed and these were broken down open by a man with an axe. Then the big pieces were taken away in a wheelbarrow or a skip to the carding room which was on the bottom floor. Next you went to the ring rooms where the mules spun long bobbins of cotton and later the smaller bobbins – which went on the shuttles in the weaving shed. As it went from machine to machine the thread got narrower. The spinners were all on piece-work so if they had a broken end they'd take the bobbin out, take the thread and twist it and make it one piece again, without stopping the machine."

Spinning cotton at Cockhedge in the mid-1950s with the majority of women clad in their working overalls and headscarves fashioned into turbans.

Many of the Cockhedge weavers were young women, and Ethel Whitfield remembers how some of them tried to keep back some of their own earnings from the family purse: "I started work at Cockhedge in 1915 at the age of 13. A lot of the men went to the war and that was my big chance to get on a machine. My first big wages were 6s [30p] and that was a lot of money then. One or two of the other workers were what we called 'flomping'. That meant helping yourself to your own money. When it was the breakfast half hour they'd say: 'How much are you flomping? I'm going to take so much out for my pocket money because I want to go to the pictures'. I had an older sister there and she knew what we got so all of my money had to be handed over to mother."

business. The trade was increasingly centred on the Cockhedge Mill, operated by Armitage & Rigby, and cotton settled down to a long and unspectacular existence as one of the many strands from which the fabric of the town's economy was woven. Its importance in providing work for women was perhaps the greatest contribution it made to the life of Victorian Warrington. Until the rise of the soap industry in the 1890s women had few other opportunities for industrial employment and since cotton, here as elsewhere in the region, represented a good steady job with above average wages it played a valuable role in the town's economic well-being. To go to Armitage & Rigby was notably better than to be in domestic service or working as a menial servant in a hotel, and what would later be a mainstay of female employment – secretarial jobs and office employment – did not yet exist.

But cotton was not the only textile trade. Here, and in some of the neighbouring villages – especially Lymm – fustian-cutting was a traditional occupation. Fustian is an all-purpose term for cloths in which two different fibres (from the 18th century, cotton and flax or linen) are woven together. It became particularly associated with cloth woven with a high looped pile, which was cut and trimmed using exceptionally long, fine, razor-sharp knives. The blade, sharp edge upwards, was run through the loops of the pile so that the threads were cut to give a soft thick nap. This contrasted with short nap cloths where the pile was trimmed horizontally using sharp shears. Fustians, of which velvet and corduroy are the best-known varieties, were usually expensive quality cloths, fetching a high price, and the cutting was a remarkably delicate and skilled operation. One mistake would ruin the perfect appearance of the finished cloth and destroy its value.

It was a labour intensive trade and employed many people. In the 1890s over 200 people in Lymm, about 20 per cent of the workforce in the village, were engaged in the fustian trade, and in 1870 Warrington town had over 60 master fustian-cutters each of whom employed several

hands. The largest firms had up to 40 cutters on the payroll, though they were paid by piecework and some worked on a casual or part-time basis. To those for whom it was their sole livelihood it meant a long and physically demanding day. We might think of hard labour as being confined to heavy industries such as mines and ironworks, but the women fustian-cutters, walking 20 miles a day from 7am to 7pm, knew well what hard work was. All damage had to be paid for and exhaustion and illness brought instant poverty. Yet the industry, because of the exceptional delicacy and skill of the task, could not be mechanised – heavy machinery was simply too crude and unresponsive to do the job as well as a trained human eye and steady hand. Not until 1911, a century and a half after mechanical power was applied to weaving and spinning, was the first practical velvet-cutting machine invented. In 1912 United Velvet Cutters opened a factory in Warrington and this quickly became the largest such concern in Britain and possibly in the world – in the mid-1930s it had a workforce of over 450. In the Edwardian period and through the 1930s, velvet was much in demand: elaborate costumes, party frocks for small girls, and endless miles of opulent curtaining ensured that the works was kept at full stretch. But wartime restrictions, post-war austerity, changing fashions and the pervasive competition from artificial fibres and fabrics spelled the end. Few people wanted velvet. In 1959 the works closed, and 250 years of fustian and velvet in Warrington had finished.

Making and finishing cloth was not an end in itself. The final stage in the textile trade was the making of clothing and furnishings. This aspect of the textile industry is almost always overlooked, yet it was extremely important. The cotton trade of Lancashire and Cheshire supported an extensive clothing sector, one which still survives tenuously in some of the cotton towns. One reason for the comparative lack of attention which it has received is that until the 1920s, when mass-produced off-the-peg clothing began to appear in the shops, a lot of clothing was made individually by self-employed workers. It is harder to track down such people in the historical record and to investigate the work which they did, but we should not underestimate their number of their role in society. After all, if we had walked down Sankey Street in 1900 just about everybody else we saw would have been stark naked if it were not for the labours of the tailors,

The older weavers trained the new entrants, as Amy Pridden who started at Cockhedge Mill at the time of World War One remembers: "I went in just as I left school at 13. I'd got my name in so I'd get the first vacancy. I was 13 weeks learning, not getting paid. A qualified weaver would eventually get four looms and you started as what they called a helper. Then you got your own two looms and if you progressed, or if there was a vacancy, then you got four. When you got four looms you were allowed a helper. You had to pay that helper but until you got on helping you did the running about for nothing. Bring the weft and run errands for what we called our 'Missus' [mistress]. We started work at six o'clock in the morning and at eight o'clock we had a breakfast half-hour. Mother used to send breakfast to the mill because she liked us to have a warm breakfast so I used to tell my mother to put in an extra bacon butty for my mistress. I got my own looms when I'd only been there 11 months, two looms for myself. When I first started as a helper I got half a crown [12½P] a week. When you got your own looms it [the wage] depended because you were on piece work, but you either used to get 11s or 12s up to 13s [55p or 60p up to 65p]."

Although the majority of the Cockhedge workforce was female, there were a number of male weavers – as well as the fitters (who kept the machinery running) and the foremen.

cutters, seamstresses and needlewomen of the town! In 1891 the census recorded 730 women and 444 men in Warrington under the heading 'clothing production', which meant that this unsung trade was the town's fifth largest employer.

This photograph (bottom) manages to capture the looms in action but cannot convey the deafening sound of the operation or the pressures on the workforce, as Amy Pridden recalls: "The noise of the mill was terrible. That's how you learned to lip read because you couldn't hear one another. The looms were very noisy and you had to shout. It was hard work learning to weave and you had to have very good eyesight. The missus showed you how to put a cop on a shuttle. You'd suck the weft thread through. The shuttle goes in a box at the end of the loom. The loom has to have a warp thread first. It's like a big rolling pin and it's covered in finger cotton. You had to thread the warp through, but the foreman helped with that because they had to bring the warp to you. You'd set your loom on and the shuttle would go backwards and forwards. You'd got to watch when the shuttle was finishing, stop your loom and put a fresh cop on. The shuttle could get trapped and make a mess of things. You'd get fined if you had a 'trap'. You wove so many yards and it was called a 'cut'. That went to the warehouse where there were pickers who examined it. They went through all of it. You had ends that sometimes broke and you'd stop your loom and piece it. If they could find out where one of those was and there were more than one or two in that piece of cloth – that was about 60 or 70 yards wide – then you'd get fined 2d or 3d. They were very strict."

Some were employed by drapery and clothing shops, where ladies and gentlemen could be measured for a garment and have it made up by tailors and seamstresses who worked behind the scenes. The larger stores had a fashion buyer whose job was to go to even larger stores in even bigger cities and copy the designs – ideally, of course, the latest London fashions – and to read the weekly journals in which drawings and plates gave details of the latest styles. These could then be advertised locally and Warrington people who wanted to cut a dash could wear the most up-to-date costumes, the latest stylish line of suiting. More prosaically, backstreet tailors and seamstresses worked long and hard to make everyday working clothes for the people of the town, where durability and cheapness, not fashion, were the essentials. Many of those boys' suits with sailor collars, workingmen's jackets and thick tough trousers, girls' pinafores and aprons, which we see in Victorian and Edwardian photographs were made up in badly-lit stuffy rooms by women and men whose eyesight was failing and whose fingers were stiff in cold winters. The census returns demonstrate that in many families the seamstresses made a vital contribution to the household budget – teenage daughters and young unmarried women for whom this was one of the few ways in which they could earn a living. To them the advent of mass-produced clothing was a disaster, even if for the people of the town it was a godsend.

As it turned out mass-produced clothing was also to become a Warrington speciality for much of the 20th century. In 1921, for example, James Bennett, the shirt and pyjama makers of Golborne Street, were advertising proudly that they produced '5,000 dozen garments each week', while the town's several shirtworks were flourishing into the 1960s. The best-known, perhaps, was MacArthur Beattie & Co, which opened in 1928, although the largest was Burton's at Wilderspool Causeway, which closed in 1977 with the loss of 630 jobs. MacArthur Beattie spent

This former fustian (or velvet) cutting shop in Manchester Road is similar to that remembered by Mrs Bradley who was born in 1906: "When I was little girl my mother and sister used to work at the velvet cutting shops. There was one up the road in Hale Street. You used to go upstairs and they used to stretch the fustian cloth along rollers and they used to walk in their bare feet. There was no electric light or gas, they had a candle at each end so they used to work by candle light. I've sat under there many a time when I was a kid; 'under the runs' they used to call it."

the war years producing uniforms for servicemen – in 1945 it proclaimed that it had turned out 1,437,900 shirts and pairs of pyjamas and 606,000 collars for the armed forces. In the 1950s the firm did well, but the movement towards mass-produced cheap shirts rather than expensive quality products, and particularly the flooding of the market with very cheap foreign imports, spelled an end to the trade.

Inside a typical velvet-cutting shop before the introduction of machinery. The fustian-cutters had to walk, hand holding the knife steady as a rock, up the line of the cloth stretched flat on a long table. By eye they guided the blade through the almost infinite number of tiny loops of thread, in the straightest of lines. At the end they stopped, reinserted the knife, and walked back again... again and again, up and down the cloth, all day and every day. Some fustian-cutters are estimated to have walked about 150 miles a week up and down the table side in the long cutting rooms. The cutting-rooms were often located in the attics of cottages or in separate workshops, as they had to have large windows to let in maximum light – dim conditions meant a far greater chance of error, and working into the night, though often needed to finish a job, was particularly hazardous.

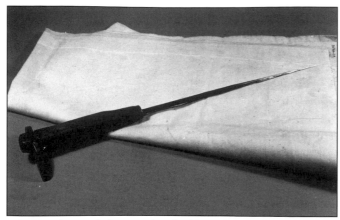

A knife used to cut the loops on the pile of fustian or velvet by hand.

The introduction of mechanised velvet-cutting had a considerable impact on the trade as this extract from a comparative Report on Livelihood and Poverty in Warrington *published in 1915 reveals: 'The trade is being revolutionised by the introduction of machinery which produces five times as much as by hand. The change will prove beneficial to the cutter. The hand-cutter will become a machine minder and will engage in less fatiguing work. At the present time the hand cutter's work results in her having to walk up and down a distance of four yards and cover in the course of a day over 20 miles. Though the girls in many cases can sit down when tired or go out for food, yet the work is very trying , especially in summer. The strain will probably in future be mental rather than physical, as the machine results in greater concentration of the mind and less physical exertion. Hand cutters start upon 4s [20p] and rise to 24s [£1.20] but only expert cutters engaged on very special work receive this high wage. The average hand cutter when working full time may be said to earn about 12s [60p] and young girls are frequently found earning this sum. With work that demands greater skill, one would naturally expect higher wages, and this is so. The machine cutter gets 5s [25p] at the age of 13 and 14 years, then after three months 7s (35p) or 8s [40p] and after six months 9s [45p]. The most efficient cutters get as high as 22s]£1.10], but the average is 14s [70p] and 15s [75p].'*

"*Meritus*"

.... HIGH GRADE

SHIRTS & PYJAMAS

Mc.ARTHUR. BEATTIE

& COMPANY LIMITED

OWEN STREET, WARRINGTON
SUPPLIERS TO WHOLESALE AND SHIPPING ONLY

Many women were employed in Warrington's shirt manufactures, including McArthur & Beattie's works seen here in an advertisement from 1948. Shirt manufactures were traditionally represented as 'sweat shops', and Mrs Cash's memories of working in Regal's works on Norman Street in the early 1920s seem to confirm the picture: "Downstairs in the laundry, dress workers were stiffening collar. That was very hot. Then you went up in the machine room and the noise was terrific. Some were doing seams, some were doing lapels, some were doing buttons, some were doing buttonholes. There were about 100-200 workers on one floor. Then up on the top floor was the cutting shop where you cut the shirts out. Added to that was the collar room where they did the collars – the loose collars. As works went it was passable."
However, Regal's later introduced a welfare scheme for their workers, representing themselves as enlightened employers: 'The factory is on the model principle with large, bright and airy rooms; and of course the usual safety devices are on the machines. Every girl is provided free with two sets of overalls and caps of different colours. Arrangements have been made with the Education Committee for young girls to attend evening schools... And a branch of the Warrington Free Library has been established at the works. A fully equipped ambulance, medical and rest room, and excellent toilet rooms have been installed. There is a large and pleasant dining hall with first-class cooking arrangements... Free tea or coffee are provided for all the workers, morning and afternoon when the works is on full time.'

Sailcloth and Shipbuilding

T HE growth of Warrington's cotton industry from the 1780s coincided with the heyday of an older textile trade, of major importance to the town and surrounding area. This was the production of sailcloth, based on locally grown flax and hemp. These two plants provide the raw materials for linen and canvas respectively, and grow particularly suitable in damp lowland areas with rich soils – ideally suited, therefore, for the damp river valleys and wetland margins of south Lancashire. Across much of the district in the 16th and 17th centuries the cultivation of flax and hemp became an important element in the agricultural economy, diversifying local farming by providing a cash crop as well as producing the raw material for domestic textile production. References to linen and canvas are found in many documentary sources in the area from 1550 onwards and it is clear that by 1650 the output of these cloths was substantial.

Processing flax and hemp was a specialised procedure. The plants were harvested (the entire plant being pulled), their roots were cut off, and then the stems and leaves were gathered into large bundles which were steeped in water for a couple of weeks, a process known as retting. This rotted the green parts of the leaves and the outer covering of the stems, making a foul-smelling greenish-brown slime, which was washed away in streams or ponds with clean water to expose the strong white or brown fibres which ran down the interior of the stem and leaves. These fibres were gathered into hanks, dried, and then heckled or scutched, which involved beating them with wooden flails so that they were broken down. Eventually a large pile of soft fluffy threads was produced and these were spun to make flaxen or hempen yarn. That could in turn be woven to make the linen or canvas cloth or mixed with other fibres, such as wool or cotton, to give different types of fabric. It was a long drawn-out

A relic of the days of one of Warrington's forgotten industries, this lead tank was formerly used in the starching of sailcloth. When Arthur Young visited the town in 1776 he found: "The manufacture of sail-cloth and sacking are very considerable. The first is spun by women and girls who earn about twopence a day. It is then bleached, which is done by men, who earn 10s [50p]a week; after bleaching it is wound by women; next it is warped by men, and then starched. The last operation is weaving, in which the men earn 9s, [45p] the women 5s [25p] and boys 3s 6d [17½p]. The sail cloth employs about 300 weavers."

business and the retting, in particular, was very disagreeable because of the stench of the rotten vegetation. It polluted water supplies and so the retting ponds were, if possible, separate from streams and watercourses. The work was seasonal and, as with many other aspects of agricultural life, women and children played their part, harvesting and gathering and in some cases helping with the washing, though the heckling, which was exceptionally strenuous, was normally done only by men. Spinning and weaving could be undertaken by men or women and in the Warrington area in the 17th and 18th centuries many homes had spinning wheels and handlooms for the production of the finished cloth. Members of the household would combine these tasks with other farming work, or even with industrial employment such as nailmaking and smithing.

Sailcloth, a particularly strong and tough canvas, became a local speciality and Warrington was nationally known as a centre for its production. Sailcloth was crucial to all shipping in the days before steam power, so the trade of Warrington not only supplied the merchant fleet but also kept the Royal going – at the end of the 18th century the Warrington district provided le than half the acreage of sails for the fleets which fought and helped to defeat Napoleon. The growth of the great port of Liverpool provided a huge local market for the sailcloth, particularly from the 1780s onwards, and Liverpool shipowners typically had standing orders from Warrington sailcloth makers. Engravings of the Liverpool docks in the early 19th century show forests of ts as hundreds of ships waited in the port, but as soon as these vessels were read to leave on a voyage they unfurled their Warrington sails. By the 1840s, though, business was in rapid decline. Industrially produced sailcloth was competing with the largely domestic production of Warrington, while the gradual extension of steam power was already having a damaging effect on overall demand. More serious than either of these, though, was the drastic 'downsizing' of the Royal Navy once the Napoleonic Wars ended in 1815. Even in the 1750s and 1760s it was recognised that when Britain was at war,

Warrington did well – the Navy was active, re-equipped, and demand was high – but when peace came Warrington suffered. After 1815 the Navy had no major active role for half a century, by which time Warrington cloth was no longer the 'cloth of choice' for naval suppliers. In 1851 the Ordnance Survey's detailed plan of the town shows just one surviving 'sailcloth manufactory', in a yard on the east side of Bridge Street. By 1870 the trade had vanished.

LIVERPOOL AND AUSTRALASIAN LINE OF PACKETS.
The under-mentioned first-class Vessels will have immediate despatch.

	Tons.	For	To sail.
TAYLEUR (new iron ship)	2000	MELBOURNE	20th Dec
SUMATRA (First Ship)	788	SYDNEY	20th Dec

Goods for Melbourne will be delivered on the Wharf, by special agreement, and will be promptly landed.—For freight &c., apply in London to Henry Hoffmann, Esq.; in Glasgow to Messrs. Dickson and Co.; or here to J. W. FAIRCLOUGH & CO., 4, Tower-buildings, West

Warrington was also a minor centre for shipbuilding. For centuries small river vessels had been constructed here, and in the early 18th century, as the scale of trade on the Mersey and the Weaver grew, output rose accordingly – but we have no detailed records to give us a clear picture of this early phase of boatbuilding. The opening of the Sankey Navigation in 1759 and the Bridgewater Canal after 1761 generated new local markets for barges, and a small boatyard was built on the Navigation just below Sankey Bridges. By the end of the 18th century the technology of shipbuilding was changing rapidly, as iron boats and steam power revolutionised the industry. Several small shipyards and repair yards were established on the river at Bank Quay and on the north bank adjacent to Warrington Bridge, where during the 1840s the Bridge Foundry constructed four iron paddle-steamers for use on the Mersey. The river here was narrow and the yard stood on one of the tight curves in its course, so this was less than ideal as a site. By this time shipbuilding was everywhere moving downriver to sites with deeper open water – thus, the Tyne, Mersey and Clyde all saw the gradual abandonment of upriver locations.

In the case of Warrington the next generation of vessels were built by Tayleur Sanderson & Co at their Bank Quay shipyard. Here the river was wider and more suitable for larger ships. Tayleurs built iron-hulled schooners for the Atlantic trade, as well as smaller steamers for passenger traffic. In 1853 they launched the largest iron ship yet constructed on the Mersey (larger than anything yet built at Birkenhead) – the clipper *Tayleur*, with accommodation for 680 passengers and designed for the long Australia runs. She was chartered by the White Star Line and caused a sensation – but an even greater sensation was her catastrophic sinking off County Dublin on her maiden voyage in January 1854. Almost 400 lives were lost and the publicity did Warrington shipbuilding no good at all. The industry continued for a time – the 1,325 ton *Sarah Palmer*, largest of all Warrington vessels, was launched in 1855 – but the average size of ships was increasing fast and Warrington, high up a difficult river and with inadequate space both for large yards and for bow-forward launching, could not compete with Birkenhead, Tyneside or Clydebank. The industry returned to its more traditional ways, and the construction of barges and small river craft continued at Sankey Bridges until the 1920s.

On 19 January 1854 the Tayleur set sail for Melbourne crowded with 660 emigrants eager to seek their fortunes in Australia. On 23 January the stunned inhabitants of Warrington heard that the ship had run aground in a storm on 21 January, just two days into her epic voyage. Some 426 of the passengers and crew perished and the survivors had harrowing tales to tell: "Wives clinging to their husbands, children to their parents... Great numbers of women jumped overboard but three women only out of 200 were saved... The ship's stern now began to sink; the ship made a lurch and all the ropes were snapped asunder...every wave washed off scores at a time; we could see them struggling for a moment, then, tossing their arms, sink to rise no more. At length the whole of the ship sank under water. There was fierce struggle for a moment and then all except two, who were in the rigging were gone... From the time the ship first struck, till she went down was not more than 20 minutes."

At the ensuing coroner's inquest the owners were held largely to blame for a number of errors, but principally for failing to realise that the Tayleur's iron hull would cause misleading compass readings which would take the ship aground. Further disasters befell the Tayleur's sister ships and to the superstitious maritime world the yard seemed jinxed. As the Bank Quay site had also proved to shallow for the launch of large vessels the boatbuilding venture soon came to an end.

An excited crowd gathered in March 1906 to witness the launch of the Santa Rosa at Clare & Ridgway's yard at Sankey Bridges. Mrs Ridgway performed the launch of this 200-ton ship which was the maximum size possible to pass through the lock at Widnes. All went well and 'the vessel slid broadways down the inclined planks, taking to the water with a fine plunge amidst the cheers of spectators'.

Ritchie & Black introduced the unlikely concept of building concrete ships to their yard at Fiddlers Ferry. Not only would the vessels actually float but the company claimed they would be ideal for the extreme atmosphere of the tropics and cheaper to produce than conventional vessels. One of their vessels is seen here under construction using similar method to that employed for a more conventional steel ship.

This completed vessel was 180 foot long and designed for a speed of nine to 10 knots at sea. She had three large cargo holds divided into five water-tight compartments with a greater capacity than either conventional timber or steel ships.

The Santa Rosa and her sister ship the Eustace Carey, launched in 1905, were built to carry chemicals for the United Alkali Company between Liverpool and other ports by coast, river and canal. Their construction marked a revival of ship building at Sankey Bridges where Clare & Son had begun business in the early 1800s as ropemakers and builders of Mersey flats.

Pínmakíng

Pictured here on the right-hand side of Knutsford Road in the early 1900s, Edelsten's Mersey Pin and Wireworks was one of Warrington's pinworks under investigation by Mr Austin for the Children's Employment Commission in the early 1840s.

AMONG the metal-working trades which developed in Warrington and adjacent villages in the years after 1700 was pinmaking. Like so many other specialised trades in the area, it required very fine and delicate work to produce tiny objects, using a high degree of skill, a perfect eye, and very nimble fingers. For this reason pinmaking, more than any other Warrington trade, became the preserve of child labour – the small fingers of children and their dextrous movements (and, in a period when only the wealthy could afford spectacles, their generally better eyesight) were more suited to this type of labour than the heavy-handed, clumsy and short-sighted adults. By the middle years of the 18th century pinmaking was tending to move from domestic production in cottages to a workshop system, where pinmakers sat in groups under the eagle eye of an overseer. It was thus halfway to the factory system, and was organised

by a small group of manufacturers who provided the raw materials and collected in the finished products. The business was gradually concentrated in the hands of the Edelsten family, who by 1820 had three separate companies (run by three brothers) which collectively controlled most of the trade and exercised a high degree of monopoly power.

Pins were made of fine wire – there was a close link with one of the town's other vital trades, wire-drawing – though for brass pins, produced in large quantities because they did not rust or produce sparks and thus more reliable for a wide range of commercial uses, a lot of the wire was brought from outside, particularly Staffordshire and Macclesfield where brass industries were well-established. The wire was made to different gauges – some pins for industrial use were fairly large, whereas the typical pin for clothing and dressmaking would be small and fine. It was delivered to the workshop in great coils and then had to be prepared. The workshop had large tables in which long pegs were firmly set. The wire was bent round the pegs time and again to make a skein, which was cut through with powerful shears to give a large bundle of pieces of the same length. These were then cut into shorter identical lengths, and cut again and again until pieces twice the length of the required pin shafts were produced. Meanwhile, using a machine, a boy would wind a long strand of ultra-fine wire around a thin brass rod to produce a long tight coil. Using small scissors he would meticulously snip off precisely two coils of the wire, so that the snippings fell into a basin – they would form the heads of the pins. A small girl would make the pins themselves. Taking two 'blank' shafts, she would thread on to each of them a tiny double curl of wire, and then place the coil end into a riveting machine. With a clap the two metal blocks of the machine came together and riveted the tiny coil of wires to the heads of the shafts. The two pins tumbled into a basin in the girl's lap, and she started again – and so it went on, for the whole of a long working day.

All contemporary observers, whether or not they approved of child labour, were of like mind in applauding the extraordinary dexterity and skill of the 'little workers'. The coils of wire were so fine, said one observer, that they resem-

John Edeltsen's grandfather had been employed as a pin-pointer in the late 18th century and by the 1840s several members of the father operated pinmaking shops around Warrington. The government enquiry described John Edelsten as 'pin manufacturer in Warrington & Latchford, at the Mersey Pinworks in the latter place for heading rooms; the warehouse, patent heading room in King Street; a heading place at Newton and sundry other heading shops in Turner's Fold and Oliver Street.'

In evidence to the enquiry he described the conditions of his workers, clearly believing himself to be a fair and concerned employer: "We employ about 400 hands altogether, principally children and young people… about 20 to 60 in a room. There are windows on each side of the rooms which they open at pleasure. The places are annually whitewashed and cleaned and warmed in winter, no heat being required only to make them comfortable… They never work more than 10 hours, exclusive of meal times, and the younger ones seldom so long. They seldom come before breakfast…. We do not knowingly allow anyone to work under the age of seven, but when the mothers bring them it is difficult to prevent it without being considered harsh."

This illustration shows a girl at work a the stamping-block where she performed the monotonous task of pin-heading.

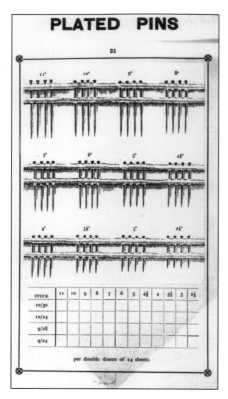

PLATED PINS

per double dozen of 24 sheets.

The next stage of pinmaking was called sheeting and involved sticking the pins into papers for sale. It was done only by girls to ensure that the papers remained clean. Austin's enquiry described the process: "The girls sit in rows at a long bench or table, with their faces to the window. On the edge of this bench and level with the breast bone, is a sort of vice and into this vice the paper which has previously been folded by the overlooker is fixed. The pins are in the children's laps in an open paper or tray. Something like a comb is used to catch them up by the heads in rows. A certain number, according to the sorts and size, are ranged on the surface of the vice, each falling into a groove made for the purpose. They are then pushed into the paper. The vice is now unclasped, one side of it is pushed against the heads of the whole row of pins, and they are thus thrust into the paper up to the head." The majority of the girls engaged in this task were aged between 10 and 14 as their hands were no longer small enough for the task of pin-heading.

Edelsten's used a variety of advertisements for their pin sheets to cope with changing tastes as Austin discovered: 'A stock of pins finished and put into papers is a precarious stock. Fashion changes even in this article, and the whole of the stock might have to be taken out of the papers and put into fresh ones. Not only a different engraving is wanted at the back of the paper, but paper of different colours, with or without gold edges: and even the number of pins to be put in a row must be altered, or the article will be unsaleable in certain markets. The pins left to themselves too will tarnish and spoil.'

bled poppy seeds. In 1841 the great majority of Warrington's child workers – 424 of about 560 workers in the town aged 5-14 years (76 per cent) – were employed in the pinmaking trade (two of them were just six years old), but the more reliable and realistic of commentators highlighted it as a particularly unhealthy or 'injurious' business. The Royal Commission which investigated child labour in several industries nationally in 1843 drew particular attention to the deplorable working conditions in which the children laboured, sitting long hours hunched over benches in smoky, hot and unventilated rooms and sheds. James Kendrick, Warrington's most prominent doctor in the 1840s and 1850s, an enlightened man with a clear reforming agenda, emphasised in his reports the long-term health problems which the child pinmakers developed – bone deformities from sitting awkwardly for so long; poor eyesight; and respiratory diseases. But it was not until the 1870s that matters began to improve. By then the employment of very small children had ceased because employment legislation and Factory Acts placed restrictions on work under 10. As a result, because its supply of cheap and nimble infant labour had dried up, the pinmaking trade was forced to experiment with mechanisation and eventually machines became a practical proposition. As a result the production of pins shifted to metal-working factories, and the backyard sheds became a thing of the past. By 1890 it was effectively dead as a trade. Hardly any physical trace of the industry remains today, for the sheds and backyard 'manufactories' have long since been swept away by redevelopment and slum clearance. Even 100 years ago, when photographers were capturing the vanishing world of late Victorian and Edwardian Warrington, there was little interest in an industry which was largely gone and the buildings were not sufficiently distinctive or remarkable to attract the attention of the photographer. Yet in its heyday pinmaking was one of the town's most important trades, and at the beginning of Victoria's reign it employed almost 1,000 people in the town. Today, like the manufacture of sailcloth, it is hardly remembered at all.

Wire

OF ALL the metal-working industries which developed in Warrington in the late 18th centuries, none was more important than wire-drawing. The industry dominated the town's employment structure in the late 19th and early 20th centuries but it, too, originated with small-scale production in backyard workshops and foundries. Unlike many metal-working trades (such as pinmaking) but like the production of hand tools and files, it expanded very rapidly and transformed into a fully-fledged factory-based industry. The reason for this impressive growth was that wire became an essential element in many other industries and in agriculture, and at Warrington – as in Sheffield and the Black Country – the manufacturers were able to capitalise on the rapid growth in the market. For example, in the 1820s and 1830s Warrington producers switched to the weaving of wire on looms (a process only made possible with the invention of the first wire-loom by James Locker in 1811). Woven wire had a very wide variety of industrial and commercial uses, particularly as the technology became more sophisticated and highly-specialised forms of wire cloth were being turned out. For instance, miners' safety lamps (including the famous design patented by Humphrey Davy) required a very fine wire gauze which allowed the flame to burn without igniting explosive gases in the atmosphere – the gauze was so fine as to resemble a soft cloth, and its production was in itself a major technical achievement. Woven wire meshes could be

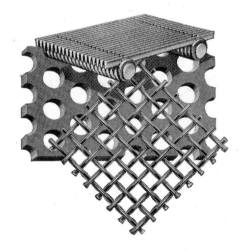

This interior shot of the Longford Wire, Iron and Steelworks in the early 20th century shows the wire drawers hard at work on their benches.

The production of spliced and stranded wire ropes continued to be a speciality of the Whitecross works as this employee demonstrates

used for sieves and riddles in commercial processes such as flour-milling, sand and gravel grading, and the production of cement, all of which were themselves growing fast during the second half of the 19th century.

In the 1880s and 1890s the widespread adoption of barbed wire in agriculture (including the expanding farming areas of the North American prairies, Australia and South Africa) provided a large new market for Warrington products. Barbed wire was a development from an earlier Victorian innovation, the manufacture of simple wire for fencing. All over Britain and beyond the use of cheap, simple and straightforward post-and-wire fencing replaced the construction of drystone walls and the planting of hedges, and every yard of wire used represented potential business for the Warrington wire-drawers. The massive increase in international trade generated huge new demands for immensely strong wire ropes and hawsers for shipping, while the expansion of coal-mining required equally formidable cables for winding gear and haulage. Thus, the Warrington industry was not only responding to industrial growth and demand, but also enabling that growth to take place. Wire is therefore especially interesting to historians because, though it was much less 'dramatic' a product than, for example, railway engines or winding gear for pitheads, it was fundamental to all manner of industries and without it they simply could not have developed in the way they did.

Wire-working was already well-established in Warrington by the 1770s, and

there is considerable evidence that it been in the town for much longer – copper and brass wire, for example, seem to have been among the products of the copperworks established at Bank Quay in the 1690s. The well-known firms which were to dominate the trade (and to exercise a powerful influence in Warrington's social, economic and political life for 150 years) appeared towards the end of the 18th century. William Houghton had a wireworks in Tanners Lane by 1775 and in 1799 Nathaniel Greening came to the town and, probably drawing upon existing know-how and expertise, set up a small factory. In 1805 he was joined by a new partner, John Rylands, whose family were originally weavers from Culcheth and who had become prominent in the sailcloth industry. Greening had the technical knowledge, Rylands had the capital to back up the expansion of his business, and in 1817 the partners moved to a new site at the end of Church Street where there was plenty of open

Two of Rylands workers
are engaged in the essen-
tial task of producing the
plate through which the
wire drawer would pull the
wire by hand on the draw
bench. The worker on the
right demonstrates
punching the holes in the
carbon steel 'wortle' plate
which the other worker
holds in place by tongs.
The wire-drawer had first
completed the skillful task
of grinding his punch to
the ideal shape for this
vital task, 'the same shape
as Blackpool Tower', as
apprentices were taught.
The plate itself was
pricked out with tapering
holes of varying gauges set
out in precise patterns in
parallel lines

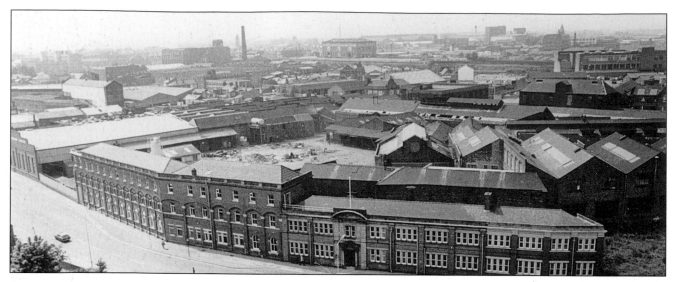

A view of Rylands operations taken from the Parish Church steeple about 1980. The impressive office block can be seen in the foreground with the Dalton Banks and Battersby Lane complex in the distance.

Even amongst the shop floor workers there was a hierarchy and in the wire industry the wire drawers were at the top of the pile as Harry Hardman recalls: "You didn't have much contact with the wire drawers because we were labouring at the time and in fact we were the great untouchables. Wire-drawers had a very privileged position in the works status. They were considered as craftsmen, they were considered to be quite a superior breed and they were key men in the wire-drawing situation. That was the craft in wire-drawing – setting the plate to the size that the customer wanted. Wire-drawers had served an apprenticeship. Craftsmen were, in that sense, very conservative and they were protecting their craft. They had a much higher standard of living than the unskilled. They were paid substantially more. When labourers were working at Rylands for about £2 2s for a 48-hour a week, the craftsmen could pick up £5-7 a week. That was an enormous difference."

land for building a 'manufactory'. Their business grew very swiftly, so that by the late 1830s the Church Street works was one of the largest industrial concerns in Warrington. In 1843 they parted company, Greening moving to new premises in Bewsey Street and Rylands retaining the Church Street site. Between them they managed to gobble up many of the smaller competitors which had started up trading in the area, though neither company was able to eliminate a later arrival, Thomas Locker (grandson of the inventor of the loom) who in 1879 began business in Market Street, and within five years had moved to a new site in Church Street and Ellesmere Street. Lockers, in particular, innovated and experimented with new uses of wire (including meshes and sieves for which they became world-renowned). In 1864 the great Whitecross works was opened by Frederick Monks, once a Rylands apprentice, and now a fierce rival of his former masters, and this, the largest and most modern of the town's works (and the only one designed from scratch on modern principles) soon employed more people

than any other Warrington factory – it had almost 1,100 employees by 1905. By 1900, therefore, Greenings, Rylands, Monks of Whitecross, and Lockers were each among Warrington's biggest companies, and collectively the wire-working trade was the most important single element in the town's economy. Such was the importance of the wire industry as a whole in the town that the original nickname of its Rugby League team – 'the Wire' – was derived from the term of 'wire-pullers'.

Wire-working was a highly-skilled and specialised business and, given its global importance and status in the town, it is not surprising that the wire-drawers themselves were the elite of Warrington's working-class community. Numerous accounts, from wire-workers themselves and from those rather lower down in the pecking order, emphasise how the wire-drawers would earn higher wages than other workers, and would proudly display their superiority – wearing suits and gold watches on chains at weekends and holidays, maintaining a lofty dignity and demonstrating a considerable contempt for 'inferior' workers, frequenting their own pubs where the prices were deliberately kept higher to keep out the lower ranks, and much-envied and perhaps much-disliked by the others. In that, perhaps, they resembled the engine drivers on the railways and the foremen and tacklers in the cotton mills, all of whom, apparently, saw

The outbreak of World War Two led to increased demand for wire in operations ranging from mine sweeping to mooring ropes for barrage balloons, for aeroplane controls, in gas masks and above all to fence off beaches from the expected invaders. Wartime demand accelerated the introduction of mechanised wire drawing and the Continuous Mill opened in Battersby Lane in 1941, with a weekly output of 1,500 tons.

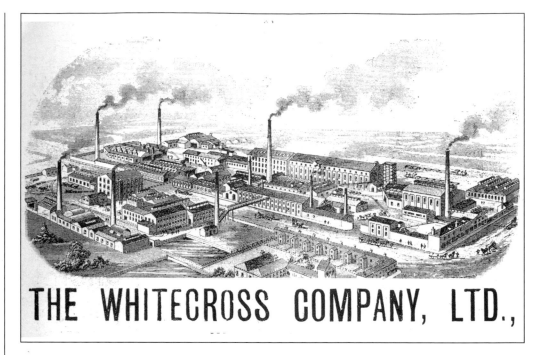

THE WHITECROSS COMPANY, LTD.,

themselves, and were seen by others, as beings who commanded and deserved the highest respect and deference. It is important to recognise that labels which are often used, such as 'working-class', are really far too simplistic and conceal much. There was a multitude of fine distinctions of grade, status, and rank within working–class society, here as in any town. An extra penny on the daily wage, a different workbench or workroom, a seemingly-trivial alteration in what we would now call 'job description', any of these could make a world of difference to people's perceptions of themselves and their jobs, to how they were viewed by others, and to where they lived and in what sort of conditions. An extra 1s 0d a week might mean that you could afford to rent a house with, say, a tiny third bedroom, or in a different and slightly superior street. These subtle differences, almost impossible to identify at 100 or more years' distance, were at the heart of the town's industrial way of life.

MECHANICAL HANDLING EQUIPMENT
AND WOVEN WIRE CONVEYOR BELTS

The British Wedge Wire Co. Ltd. - Warrington - England

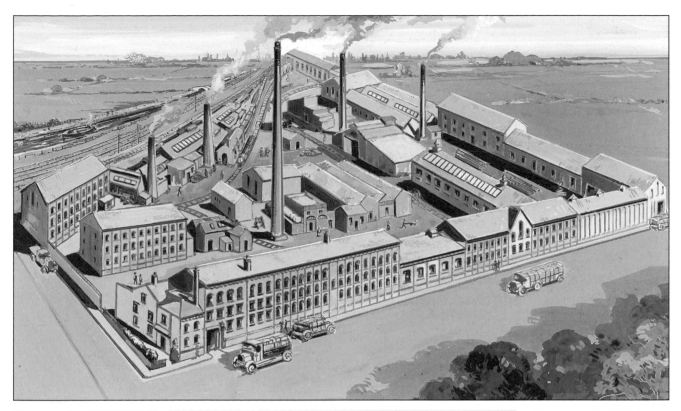

The Sankey Wire Mills, Wire Rope and Bright Steel Barworks of W. D. Houghton, which also specialised in wire rope production as well as the finer Bull Brand piano wire.

This forklift truck driver from the Firth Wire Company may have been on a proper training course but learning on the job tended to be the norm in the 1960s. Manoeuvring the truck could prove tricky as David discovered whilst working in a wire factory at Cockhedge: "Behind where Carpet World is now was Armitage & Rigby's factory and a little narrow cobbled lane and old terraced houses where the workers lived. We had a little warehouse there with coils of wire all stacked up. I'm going down [the lane] with four coils of wire on the truck bouncing on this cobbled road and it's a winter's day and it's going dark. There's no licence on this truck – they didn't bother. There's no lights on this truck! I hit the cobbles, one of the coils on the front bounced off and the wheel of the truck went into the hole in the coil. So, I'm stuck in the middle of the road! They came dashing out of the works and brought six blokes with levers trying to prise the forks up to get this roll out, while the manager's stood on the street corner looking out for the local bobby!"

The Firth Wire Company proudly displays its products on Stand 1103 in 'The Palace of Engineering' at the British Empire Exhibition of 1926 (the event which gave English football the old Wembley Stadium).

The Firth Company's intrepid band of fitters takes a well-earned break from keeping the machines of the wire industry running.

This late 20th-century photograph shows the production process for Rylands trademark Rylink fencing.

A 1948 trade advertisement for Locker's products which became the only survivor of Warrington's wire-weaving firms in the 21st century.

Heavy Metal

WITH the development of its metal-using industries, Warrington needed supplies of iron on a large scale. All of it had to be brought from elsewhere, since the town had never produced iron. There are no local supplies of ore, and although the coalfield is close by the water (essential as a power source in all early ironmaking areas) power was also limited. In the 18th century the nearest sources of iron were the Wigan area (where there were forges and small foundries using thin beds of ore occurring in the coal measures) and mid-Cheshire. Warrington imported large quantities of bar iron (that is, iron which had been smelted and cast in bars ready for reworking) and there were a number of slitting mills, in which the bars were cut into useable forms. One of the best-known was the Lymm slitting mill, on the Bradley Brook in the centre of the village, a water-powered mill operating from the 1620s onwards. Here bars were slit for nailmaking and later for making metal hoops for the wooden barrels used in the short-lived gunpowder works at Thelwall.

In this area, as in other industrial districts without local ore, there was a heavy reliance on imported metal, but also pressure by the early 19th century to develop a local iron industry to supply the needs of firms in the vicinity. The opening of the canal and railway networks meant that iron and steel could readily be brought from further afield – by 1860 Warrington companies were using steel from Barrow in Furness, Teesside and the Sheffield-Rotherham area, among others – but, given the large local demand, the possibility of producing

This mid-1930s advertisement for Forshaw & Son neatly illustrates many of the processes which were carried out in the numerous Warrington firms involved in the production of iron and steel goods.

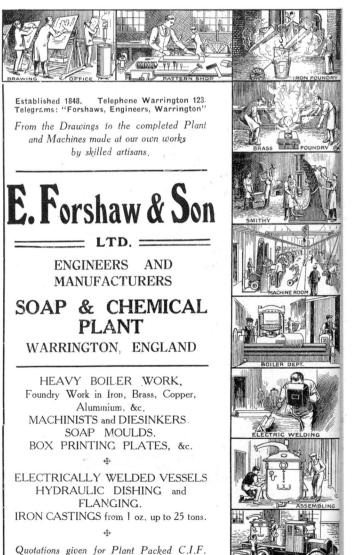

Established 1848.   Telephone Warrington 123.
Telegrams: "Forshaws, Engineers, Warrington"

From the Drawings to the completed Plant and Machines made at our own works by skilled artisans.

E. Forshaw & Son

LTD.

ENGINEERS AND MANUFACTURERS

SOAP & CHEMICAL PLANT

WARRINGTON, ENGLAND

HEAVY BOILER WORK.
Foundry Work in Iron, Brass, Copper, Aluminium, &c.
MACHINISTS and DIESINKERS.
SOAP MOULDS.
BOX PRINTING PLATES, &c.

ELECTRICALLY WELDED VESSELS
HYDRAULIC DISHING and FLANGING.
IRON CASTINGS from 1 oz. up to 25 tons.

Quotations given for Plant Packed C.I.F. Own Port.

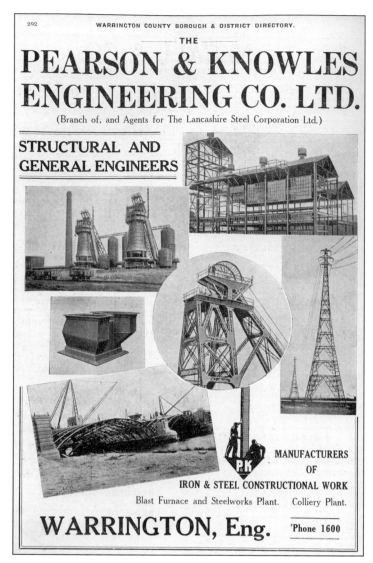

By the time of this 1935 trade advertisement, Pearson & Knowles (or P & K as it was popularly known) had been formed by the amalgamation of three major local companies and had found a market in supplying many new civil engineering projects.

it on the spot was attractive. Though it did not have raw materials Warrington had obvious potential because of the excellence of its location and transport links. Thus, a town seemingly without the conditions to develop an iron industry turned into a significant producer. The first ironworks was the Dallam Forge, opened in 1845 by William Neild, Henry Bleckly and Thomas Fell. That was just after the opening of the main north-south railway line through Bank Quay, an event which changed the economics of the enterprise and for the first time made it viable to use the new and efficient transport links for the importing of raw materials (mainly pig iron produced elsewhere, at smelters on the iron orefields such as Furness and Scunthorpe). Thus, Warrington's ironworks were involved in the second stage, processing the pig iron into a more finished form. The new industry soon developed very close ties with wireworking and hand tool firms in particular.

In the mid-1860s two new firms, the Dallam Forge Company and the Warrington Wire Iron Company, were formed with the specific aim of producing the bars, sheets, rods and hoops of iron so essential to the town's industries. In 1874 the two companies amalgamated with a major Wigan colliery company to form Pearson & Knowles Coal and Iron Company. Thus enlarged, Pearson & Knowles began to specialise in supplying a guaranteed local market – it did not produce much bar iron and its 'general' sales were relatively small, but it capitalised on the vigour of the industries of Warrington and the surrounding area to provide exactly what the customer wanted. At the same time it exploited the fact that one of its directors, Thomas Knowles, was a director of the London & North Western Railway Company. Pearson & Knowles secured valuable contracts for the casting of bridge girders, locomotive wheels and axles (3000 pairs of these a week by 1908) and valves, tubes, tanks and castings.

In 1874 Frederick Monks, the wire-drawer, opened Warrington's second major ironworks on the north bank of the river at Atherton's Quay. This eventually extended for almost a mile along the riverside, served not only by its own wharves (and its own vessels as well) but also by a network of sidings running off the Warrington-Widnes railway. Monks went into partnership with his brother-in-law, William Hall, and, as Monks Hall & Co, the company eventually became one of the world's greatest producers of finished iron and steel, with forge mills, puddling furnaces, welding works, a tube works and a riveting plant. Here, too, the semi-processed iron was brought in from elsewhere and then recast into workable form, producing sheet iron, bars, tubes, rods and plate for a wide variety of local industries and for firms elsewhere in north-west England. By 1914 it had also developed a large export market, particularly to the Continent.

Frederick Monks was not only the founder of one of Warrington's leading iron and steelworks but he also played an important role in local politics, serving on the town council from its creation in 1847.

Thus, Warrington, not an obvious place for an iron industry, eventually became one of Britain's leading centres in this essential sector of industrial output. Clearly the huge demand of local metal-working trades (and especially wire-working) was primarily responsible for this, but the presence of the Dallam and Monks Hall complexes itself created new industries. For example, the production of bedsteads, mattresses, cookers and ranges, each of which was a major employer in the town by 1900, was directly the result of the ready access to prepared wire coils and sheet iron. Monks Hall, in particular, serves as a reminder of the way that inter-relationships flourished between the different industries, each playing its part in maintaining economic diversity but many of them involved in the same overall production process, using each other's products and often controlled by the same 'umbrella' firms or members of the same families. From pins and tiny watch springs, through cookers and mattress coils, to steel girders and railway engine parts, the enormously wide range of Warrington's metal-working trades reflected late Victorian and Edwardian industrial society in all its many aspects.

Life in the ironworks was famously hard. This was heavy industry in the true sense, with fearsomely difficult manual labour, massive (and to modern perceptions acutely dangerous) machinery on a grand scale, intense heat and noise, flying sparks, white-hot metal being poured from giant ladles, huge sheets and girders being shifted around the works and loaded and unloaded from ships and wagons, often by human effort. It was the very antithesis of the minutely-detailed processes involved in, for example, the making of pins or the fine cutting of the small files used in delicate industrial processes. Yet they were two ends of the same spectrum, the common denominator being metal and its working and processing.

On Warrington Walking Day, 28 June 1895, Councillor Frederick Monks (the bearded figure seen here with the top hat) became a major benefactor to the town when he presented the ornate cast-iron gates which now grace Warrington's Town Hall. Originally designed for an international exhibition of 1862, and potentially for Queen Victoria's Sandringham home, the gates had languished at the factory for many years until ironmaster Monks had purchased them as an appropriate replacement for the ugly brick wall which hid the council's headquarters.

This early industrial photograph by fellow town councillor Thomas Birtles shows the scale of Monks Hall & Co's operation by the end of the 19th century.

All day long an incessant clatter could be heard from the Hot Rivetworks at Monks Hall. This 1970s photograph shows the straight rods being taken from the furnace by Edward Howey and fed into a shear. Stan Beddard (to his left) picks up the hot pieces and places them in the rivet dies

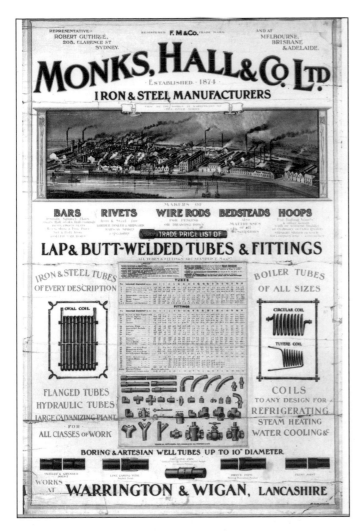

Meanwhile in the Cold Rivet Shop at Monks Hall, seven machines were also hard at work. Number 7 machine is running in the foreground whilst Geoff Mullen is fixing a new coil on to Number 6 machine. In the background Ken Furby adjusts Number 5 machine.

Number 4 machine has finished its operation in the Cold Rivet shop and Ken Furby picks up the finished rivets for bagging.

Foreman engineer John Coleman, who had worked at Monks Hall for 38 years, operates a planing machine to sharpen a blade for Number 5 Mill shears.

A last long look at Number 5 Rolling Mill taken shortly before its closure in February 1986 by a Warrington Museum photographer who had been asked to record the last days of the traditional hand-rolling process at Monks Hall. Seen from the overhead crane, this shot shows most of the mill – from the cooling beds in the foreground to the furnace at the far end.

After 30 years' service at Monks Hall, blacksmith Dennis Clark makes a final pair of box tongs for use in the mill.

Standing outside the roller's cabin in Monks Hall's Number 5 Rolling Mill in 1970, foreman Jimmy Hamlett would have appreciated the technicalities of the operation going on about him. At the time the mill was rolling angles. In the background on the left was the oil-fired furnace and then the Bolting Rolls, then directly in line was the Inters and then the Finishing Train. Seen from the left were the Strand Rolls, the Oval Edgers and then the Finishers.

The white-hot bars travel along the driven roller track of the 1st and 2nd Roughing Rolls in Number 4 Mill, Monks Hall.

A long view of the finishing train as the white hot metal emerges from the furnace in the background.

A view of the finishing train at Monks Hall as the bars are put into the billet rolls in the foreground

Life in an iron and steelworks was famously hard. This was heavy industry in the true sense, with fearsomely difficult manual labour; massive, and to modern perceptions acutely dangerous machinery on a grand scale; intense heat and noise; flying sparks and, above all, white-hot metal.

A view of the inspection bench of Monks Hall's Number 5 Mill warehouse where quality controller Barry Hampson uses a spark tester to inspect a potentially faulty bar whilst Number 5 Mill's day-inspector, Steve Ellison, looks on.

In 1913 The British Aluminium Company brought another branch of the metal industry to Warrington when they opened their Bank Quay plant. This new lightweight metal was better suited for many of the advances of a new century than its traditional competitors, although it was formed by common metal-working techniques. In this 1946 photograph the women are hard at work in the foreground at the draw benches which pulled out the metal through dies to the required shape.

Peter Spilsbury (on the right on the front row) worked at British Aluminium between 1955 and 1960, serving his apprenticeship there. "Typically any laborious or dirty jobs were usually assigned to us apprentices. One old skill that's now gone was mending the belts that were on the line-shafts that drove the machinery... Whenever I see an old photograph of a factory showing the belt system, in my mind I can still hear the cry: 'The belt's snapped, get the lad on it!' Another dirty job was when the hot dies had been put through the whale oil tank to temper the metal. After they had been in the tank overnight to cool we were told to get them out. The tank was arm-length in depth. We had to roll up our overall sleeves as far as we could then put our arm in the tank and feel around to find the dies. The smell of the oil was foul and we spent much of the day washing our arms trying to get rid of the smell."

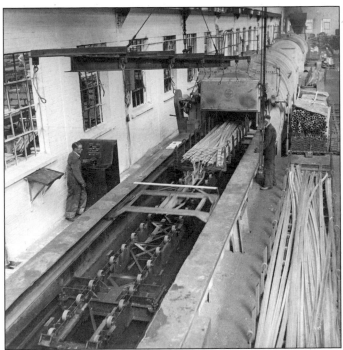

Peter Spilsbury describes how these women pointed the ends of the aluminium rod ready to go through the former: "You pass it from the die and pull it through. You had to make a cone at the end [of the rod] and by putting that in there it would squeeze the ends in. I think you can see it on some of these – made like the end of a pencil, and then that's put through the former, grabbed with the tongs and could be circle, square whatever you want. The women worked very hard and they all got a bit less pay – which to me was wrong."

Here a section rolls out of the heat treatment- furnace in the extrusion plant at British Aluminium with no danger to the workers – but there were hazards attached to other processes. Peter Spilsbury recalls the degreasing of the aluminium. "If you want it really clean you put it in there in a chemical, potent stuff. When it was first introduced well we were all unaware that the vapours could make you ill and the chap in charge of the tank used to sing for hours. It's only when he got too much of it he found out what it was. We knew he was high when he started singing!"

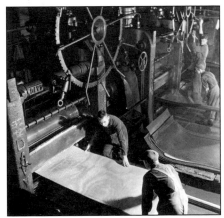

The process of sheet rolling aluminium was very labour intensive, as Peter Spilsbury explains: "You've got two men there and two on the other side. You've got sheet aluminium after rolling it and you pass it through the roll and the men would pass it back over, turn the wheel, move it down a bit more and keep going until they got it the thickness they wanted. You roll the gauze and aluminium together to start it through, and then as it rolls through it imprints the metal with a pattern. Usually it's very glossy aluminium like flooring or panelling. They would probably come from Babcock & Wilcox round the Bridge Foot area or Locker's, they made that kind of thing."

British Aluminium workers took part in a BBC radio broadcast Works Wonders *from the canteen on 11 January 1950.*

Making a Brave New World

A newly-made wire mattress withstands the 'One-Ton Mattress' test at the Longford Wire, Iron & Steelworks. A selection of the company's elaborate iron-framed bedsteads can also be seen in the background. Their light tubular construction made them ideally suited to manoeuvre up the narrow stairs of small terraced houses, particularly if they could be dismantled and reassembled on site.

INDUSTRIAL history tends to be selective. The books tell us all we need to know about some industries – cotton and wool, coal and railway engines – and overlook areas of work which were essential to everybody's lives. We ourselves forget the everyday, unglamorous items which make our lives more comfortable than those of our ancestors. Two of Warrington's industries in the early 20th century made just such ordinary products, yet they transformed the lives of millions of people. We now take them for granted, but these industries in their day brought genuine progress and made life easier for households up and down the land. Take, for example, the manufacturing of bedsteads and mattresses. We spend a third of our lives in bed and even when the working day was so much longer people would spend a quarter of the time there. Yet until the early 19th century few people slept on an iron or brass bedstead – most had wooden beds and the very poor had no beds at all. Comfort depended on the thickness of the mattress and the quality of feathers you could afford (goose, duck, even chicken) or on the volume of straw and chaff stuffed into a sacking bag.

The invention of the sprung mattress was truly a revolution in domestic comfort. Based on a large number of tightly-tensioned and immensely strong metal springs, it was made possible by improvements in technology. The wire had to be made of exceptionally resilient toughened steel, and it was impossible to produce them by hand, while the special steels themselves were not perfected until the early 19th century. Thereafter sleeping arrangements were changed beyond recognition. You no longer had to have enormously thick layers of bedding UNDER you if you wanted a good night's sleep (remember the old fable of the princess and the pea?). But the new mattresses were not the only improve-

Joyce Lister remembers working in the spring mattress department of Monks Hall in the early 1950s. "I worked in the lacing department. Down below there was Diamond where they made the diamond mattresses and wove the spring mattresses. These were not the spring mattresses we know now but flat mattresses made with spring wire – and people put a feather or a flock bed on top of them. Here they are actually making the spring mattresses and, when they'd finished weaving them, the mattresses came up to the top department where I worked." Joyce Lister left Monks Hall after about four years and the mattress department finally closed in 1964 as spring interior mattresses came into fashion.

ment. The sophisticated ways of producing steel, brass and iron products also included the ability to make relatively light iron frames for beds and, by the mid-19th century, hollow tubings which allowed great strength but little overall weight. The classic late Victorian brass bedstead, and its poorer relation the iron bed, were born.

Warrington specialised in the production of bedsteads and mattresses, as a spin-off from the existing metal-working trades and by the late 1860s using the output of the new ironworks. Monks Hall & Co had a separate bedstead works within the great complex of industrial buildings on the riverside at Atherton's Quay, large enough to be separately named on the Ordnance Survey maps. By 1900 it was one of the country's largest manufacturers of bedsteads. The Firth Company, founded in 1883 at Firth Place off Froghall Lane, acquired the Florence wiremills at Howley in 1895. Although the company originally produced a wide

"This is the lacing department. We threaded a rod through the end of the spring mattress and laced the end of the wires over the rod using a pair of pliers. You had one pair of pliers for cutting the ends off and then a pointed pair of pliers to lace over the rod. I was 17 when I started at Monks Hall in 1949 and they gave you another lady to work with. You soon picked the job up, it was monotonous really."

range of wire goods, including gauzes, cloths and screens, it began to concentrate on mattresses and in the early 20th century was one of the world's leading producers, with a global market. British colonial administrators slept on Firth mattresses in India and Central America, settlers in the veld of Southern Africa and the Australian outback settled down at night to a comfortable (if hot) night's sleep on the products of Warrington's industries!

Meanwhile, daytime domesticity was being

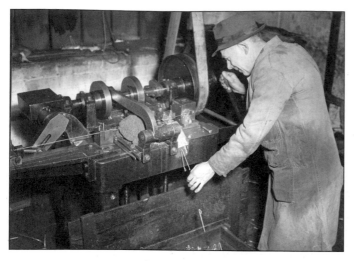

"This is the foreman in the diamond mattress section. He's making the wires for the diamond mattress and then they go to the girls."

"Here they are making the diamond mattress which is hanging down from a frame. What they did was to thread the wires the man had made on to a machine and turn the ends over to lock them together with pliers."

transformed by Warrington ingenuity. In the late 18th century the domestic fire was still the standard means of cooking for most ordinary households, either as an open hearth or in a very basic 'hob', a metal box with bars across the front. Hardly anybody except the wealthy had an oven, and only the upper- and middle-class households had sophisticated cooking equipment and facilities. By the 1820s the kitchen range, as it was later to be understood, was found in many ordinary households and from the 1840s, as industrial and urban development spread across the north of England and hundreds of thousands of terraced houses were built, major new demand was generated. By the 1880s a range, usually with an open fire, hotplate, built-in oven and water-heater, was a standard fitting in every newly-built kitchen, and many of these were being manufactured using iron plate produced in Warrington. By this time, though, the gas cooker had been invented and gas undertakings were promoting this as the cooking medium of the future. In 1890 E.W.T. Richmond founded a gas cooker business in Academy Street, Warrington. The timing was perfect, for the kitchen range – which only 30 years earlier was the modern way of doing things – was increasingly regarded as old-fashioned, dirty, and difficult to use. After only three months' Richmond's business had outgrown its premises and the business moved to Scotland Road, where it grew with remarkable speed – within

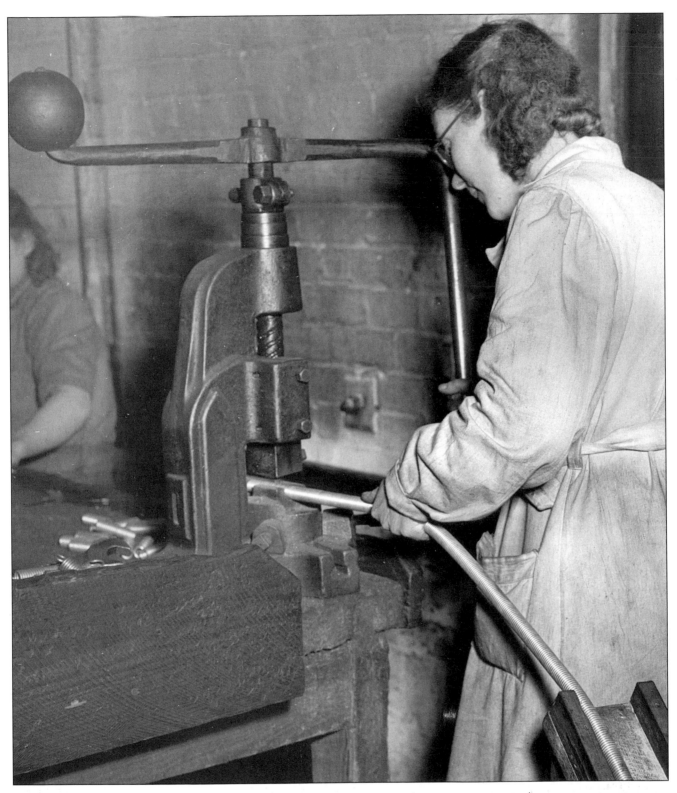

six years it employed almost 500 people – and in 1906 the company, now one of the half dozen leading cooker manufacturers in Britain, moved to its Latchford site where there was plenty of room for further expansion.

A rival had appeared. The output of Fletcher Russell's works at Wilderspool Causeway was also growing rapidly, for the gas companies were making ever more attractive offers to potential consumers and – crucially – the price of gas fell sharply so that it became extremely competitive as a fuel for heating, lighting and cooking. Both firms produced not only gas stoves but also water-heaters, gas

"This is making the springs that would go on the end of the diamond mattress. She's got the length of coil and she cuts it to make the small springs."

"Here Eileen Cooper turns the little loop on the end of the spring that would link into the bed irons. That's all she did all day long."

fires and gas irons. Between 1919 and 1921 they and four other companies amalgamated to produce a single group, Radiation Limited, which had a controlling interest in the British domestic cooker market. Rationalisation took place and eventually the production of cookers was concentrated in Warrington, where the famous name 'New World' was registered as a trademark in 1926. At that time persuasive advertising was widening the variety and choice of cookers, and they were affordable by almost any household – in 1928, for example, a New World Bungalow cooker (the word 'bungalow' at this time stood for 'small, neat and compact') cost just £23 2s 6d [£23 12½p], and for an extra £3 5s you could have one with an all-enamel finish, a godsend to housewives whose life had been spent scrubbing and scouring and scraping to get the old coal-fired range spotless. Indeed, the enamelling of cookers became one of the symbols of the modern age – it was a brand-new process, gave a smooth, clean and shiny finish, was hard-wearing and durable, and allowed colours (usually creams or the

Many of Fletcher Russell's coal-fired ranges were installed in Warrington's council housing estates which were springing up in the 1920s and 30s in nearby Latchford and Westy. They not only heated the house but also provided hot water for the new bathroom as well as a small oven for cooking and baking.

The "MODERN" COAL RANGE.

The Latest Type of Range, specially suitable for Bungalows, Housing Schemes and Subsidy Houses.

Many other patterns and types of Ranges, also Mantels, Mantel Registers, Interiors, etc.

Manufactured and Supplied by

FLETCHER, RUSSELL & CO., LTD.
RADIATION LTD., Proprietors
PALATINE WORKS, WARRINGTON

distinctive black and white mottled finish) which gave an instant light bright feel to a kitchen. What seems to us so commonplace and ordinary, something we take for granted, was to families 80 years ago a transformation of their living conditions and domestic labours. A cooker which was clean, with heat regulation, a plate rack, an oven, heat at the turn of a handle rather than after carrying the coal and stoking and raking ... that really was progress, and if you think about it, it seems so even now.

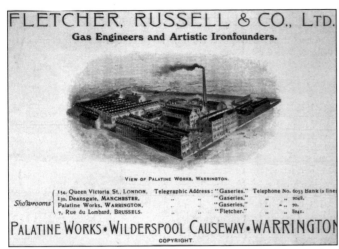

Fletcher & Russell & Co's extensive Palatine works grew out of an amalgamation in 1892 between the firms of Thomas Fletcher, a dentist, who had turned a hobby of making gas appliances for his own home into a business, and Russell's iron foundry of Manchester who made Fletcher's castings. Their new premises on Wilderspool Causeway had private railway sidings, imposing offices, a drawing office where new products were developed, chemical laboratories and extensive showrooms as well as the factory areas.

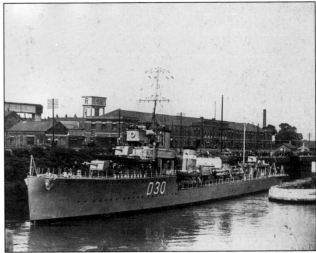

Richmond's new works by Latchford Locks on the Manchester Ship Canal were equally imposing as a local trade directory explained: 'The foundry is one of the largest of its kind in the North of England, with a daily output of between 40 to 50 tons of castings. The Enamelling Department is also the largest and the finest of its kind. The vogue of the grey mottled and also of the blue enamelled cooker has necessitated tremendous developments in this section of Grappenhall Works. A highly-trained staff, using entirely new plant and extensive methods of production are constantly employed upon the manufacture of New World cookers in Rado enamelled finish. The grinding shops, the sand-blasting shops, machine shops, assembling shops, tin smiths' shops; water heating department, the department devoted to the manufacture of hotel cooking equipment; the Gasfire Radiantmaking shop, the Warehouse with its complete system of overhead runways for the speedy movement of goods; the facilities for packing, despatch and transport- these are only a selected list of departments which comprise the vast organisation of which Warrington is so justly proud.'

The entrance to Richmonds' works with the gatekeeper's lodge where the workers clocked in and left their pay tally.

Workers from Richmond's Moulding shop in the 1920s pose with some examples of their output.

The staff of Richmond's Chandos Department poses for an official photo-graph in the 1920s. Jim Coyne remembers working there at the time: "I've worked in foundries most of my life – coremaking. I went to Richmond's on regular nights at the age of 62. I was put in charge of the women coremakers 6pm until 10pm and then went in the Chandos inspecting until 6 o'clock in the morning, a 12-hour shift. The Chandos was where they did the enamelling of all these gas cooker parts."

This view (right) shows the all-important ovens used to fire the enamelled castings in the Chandos. Walter Norris recalls working there in the 1930s: "Only one department was on shift work and that was the enamelling department. When I started working at Richmonds I clocked on at half past five and if you were late you were quartered. With overtime you could get nine or 10 hours in. The enamelling department was the worst paid for a man. The top rate then in the 1930s was about £2. And 16s for an apprentice sheet metal worker."

Young workers at Richmond's works.

The predominantly female workforce of the core shop prepare the ceramic cores for the radiants for firing

Gas fire radiants are tightly packed ready for firing.

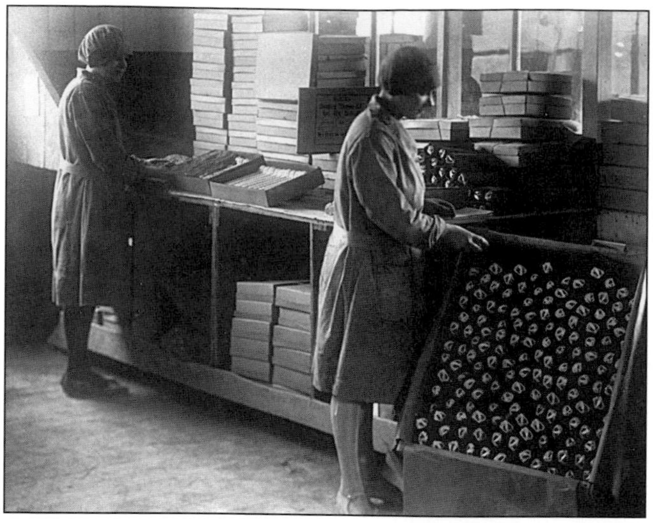

The completed gas fire radiants are carefully packed for distribution to the customers.

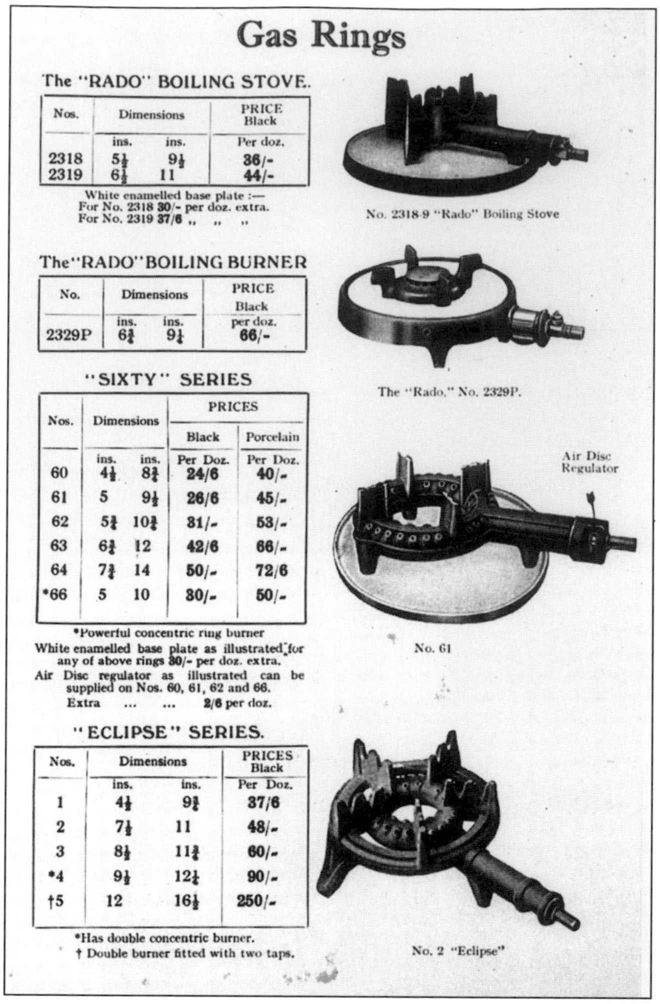

Gas Rings

The "RADO" BOILING STOVE.

Nos.	Dimensions		PRICE Black
	ins.	ins.	Per doz.
2318	5½	9½	36/-
2319	6½	11	44/-

White enamelled base plate :—
For No. 2318 30/- per doz. extra.
For No. 2319 37/6 " " "

No. 2318-9 "Rado" Boiling Stove

The "RADO" BOILING BURNER

No.	Dimensions		PRICE Black
	ins.	ins.	per doz.
2329P	6¾	9¼	66/-

The "Rado," No. 2329P.

"SIXTY" SERIES

Nos.	Dimensions		PRICES	
			Black	Porcelain
	ins.	ins.	Per Doz.	Per Doz.
60	4½	8¾	24/6	40/-
61	5	9½	26/6	45/-
62	5¾	10¾	31/-	53/-
63	6¾	12	42/6	66/-
64	7¾	14	50/-	72/6
*66	5	10	30/-	50/-

*Powerful concentric ring burner

White enamelled base plate as illustrated for any of above rings 30/- per doz. extra.

Air Disc regulator as illustrated can be supplied on Nos. 60, 61, 62 and 66.
Extra ... ... 2/6 per doz.

Air Disc Regulator

No. 61

"ECLIPSE" SERIES.

Nos.	Dimensions		PRICES Black
	ins.	ins.	Per Doz.
1	4½	9¾	37/6
2	7½	11	48/-
3	8½	11¾	60/-
*4	9½	12¼	90/-
†5	12	16½	250/-

*Has double concentric burner.
† Double burner fitted with two taps.

No. 2 "Eclipse"

For many working-class families in the early 20th century, gas was used for lighting their terraced house and the coal-fired range was usually used for cooking. The house's narrow gas pipe could be used to power a small ring to boil pans in the tiny scullery.

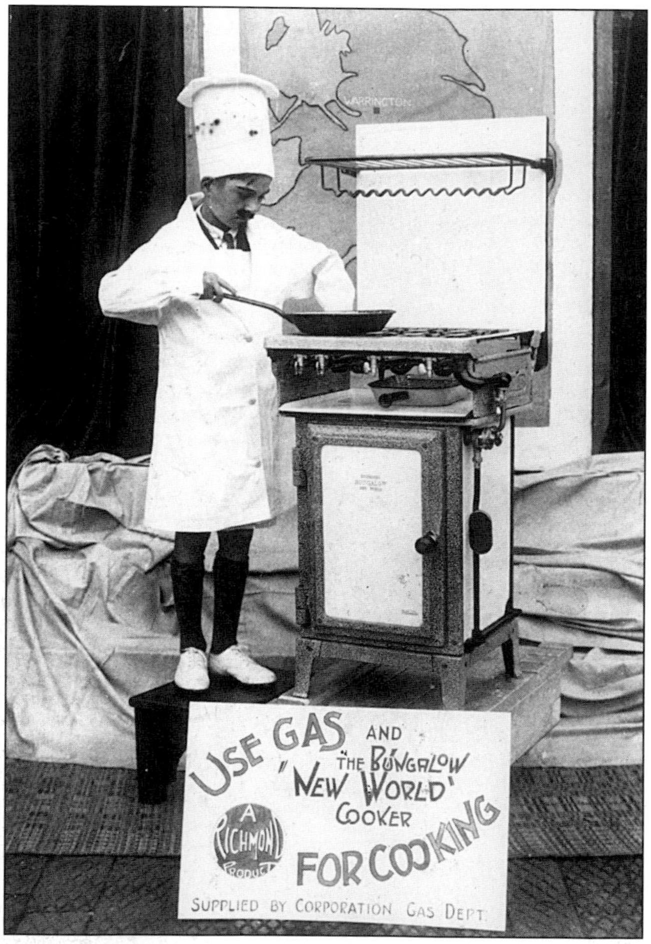
WARRINGTON
USE GAS AND THE BUNGALOW 'NEW WORLD' COOKER FOR COOKING
A RICHMOND PRODUCT
SUPPLIED BY CORPORATION GAS DEPT.

This budding chef from Silver Street School was taking part in a special Mother's Day presentation in 1930 and Warrington Corporation Gas Department had lent one of their stock of Richmond's gas cookers for the occasion. The New World Bungalow cooker, was typical of gas stoves of the period; sturdily made, with a grey-mottled stove-enamelled frame and white splash back for the grill. On the right of the cooker is the taper which was used to light the grill and the oven which was controlled by Richmond's patented Regulo.

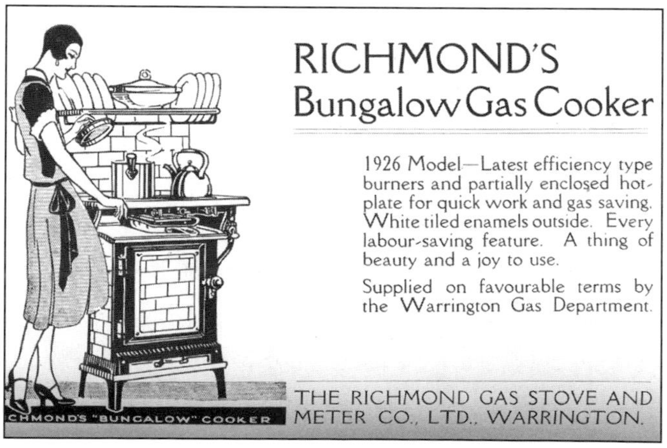
RICHMOND'S
Bungalow Gas Cooker
1926 Model—Latest efficiency type burners and partially enclosed hot-plate for quick work and gas saving. White tiled enamels outside. Every labour-saving feature. A thing of beauty and a joy to use.
Supplied on favourable terms by the Warrington Gas Department.
CHMOND'S "BUNGALOW" COOKER
THE RICHMOND GAS STOVE AND METER CO., LTD., WARRINGTON.

Glass

IN THE 16th century glass was a rare commodity in England. It was not produced in this country and all glass had to be imported, usually from the Low Countries. During the Tudor period the technology of glassmaking was reintroduced, particularly by refugees from religious persecution on the Continent, and a flourishing industry developed in the Weald of Surrey and Sussex. The crucial ingredient for glassmaking was silica, obtainable as pure sand, and the location of the industry was – as it would be for another three centuries – determined largely by the availability of that essential material. Other key elements included fireclay, needed for the crucibles since glassmaking requires exceptionally high temperatures, and fuel for the furnaces. During the later 16th century other glassmaking sites appeared, including several in northern England. By the late 17th century glassmaking was becoming more widespread – prices were falling and demand was growing, while the dawning consumer age generated a new market for drinking glasses, bottles, vases and of course window panes.

By 1695 a glassworks had been opened at Bank Quay – Warrington's first, and in the long-term most important, industrial area. Virtually nothing is known of the glassworks' history, but it is clear that it was short-lived. The owner of the works, John Leaf (or Leafe), soon moved to St Helens and at Thatto Heath established the first works in the town which was destined to become the world's most important centre for glass-making by the end of the 19th century. In 1757, however, Peter Seaman opened a flint glass works in Orford Lane (ground flint was an alternative source of silica and gave a glass of specially high quality, but the grinding process added consider-ably to overall costs). Seaman died in 1788 and the works was taken over by a partnership which had extensive interests in another glassmaking

Glassmaking at Warrington in the late 18th (or very early 19th century), as shown by local artist James Cranke. The scene was probably painted at the Bank Quay Glassworks and shows the skilled glassblower in his 'chair' shaping the molten glass with the tools which are set out around him. The younger worker in the foreground may have been his apprentice.

This early drawing conveys the feverish activity of Warrington glass-blowers at work, with the young boys learning their trade; the older 'taker-in' heating up the glass in the oven in the background and the experienced hands blowing the bowls of a glass before shaping it and attaching the stem and foot.

area, Stourbridge near Birmingham. Other glass-works were opened in the town in the same period, including the Perrin family works at Bank Quay (1765) which produced coloured and painted glassware. It is important to remember that although St Helens eventually came almost to monopolise production in north-west England, it was originally just one of the host of glassmaking towns including Liverpool, Manchester, Salford, Atherton, Newton le Willows and Warrington itself, for example. Indeed, in the 1770s, just before the great Ravenhead Works was founded, Warrington probably had more glass producers than St Helens itself.

By 1828, when detailed lists of makers begin to appear in trade directories, Warrington had six major glasshouses, including Alderson, Perrin & Robinson, successors of the original Perrin works at Bank Quay – they were now located at

There were three main sites for glassmaking in Warrington in the 19th century. The earliest was the Bank Quay Glassworks – established by Peter Seaman in 1757 and subsequently operated by Josiah Perrin and Perrin & Geddes & Co. In the late 1860s a second, and separate, operation, known as the Mersey Glassworks, was begun by Robinson's, possibly Warrington's best-known firm. There were also two glassworks at Cockhedge with the Crown Glassworks producing window glass and the Cockhedge Glassworks, whose proprietors included Alderson, Perrin and Robinson. The final site was at Orford Lane, whose early operators also included the Robinson family. Only Robinson's Mersey Glassworks survived into the 20th century.

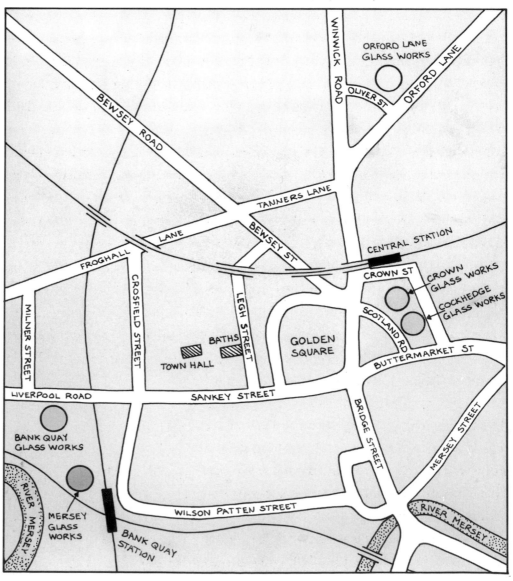

Cockhedge and as well as producing flint glass they, like many other Warrington firms, had identified a market niche which they made their own, for they were producers of the very delicate watchglasses supplied to the watch and clock makers in the town and in centres such as Prescot and Newton. Warrington, though, lacked some of the essential elements which explain the success of St Helens. The latter was sitting on top of a rich coalfield and – equally important – thick deposits of very pure marine sand, known geologically as the Shirdley Hill sands, which extended northwards through Windle to Rainford and Skelmersdale. The essential raw material was therefore on the spot. Just as important was that the St Helens industry was technically more innovative (notably in developing plate-glass casting, introduced from France in the late 1760s and perfected at the new Ravenhead works in 1774). Technical innovation was extremely costly, and the St Helens firms were, for a variety of reasons, better funded and had a stronger financial base. Crown glass (where the molten glass is blown into a pear shape and then rotated very rapidly to spin it out into a flat glowing disc) was more labour intensive and could only produce small sheets of glass, whereas plate glass (where the molten glass was poured on to a huge iron table and rolled into a sheet) allowed much larger pieces to be manufactured. The typical plate glass works involved a huge vaulted brick hall, with great tank furnaces. In contrast the older crown glass works, which were of the sort found in Warrington, had smaller furnaces and were characterised by the distinctive conical furnace towers seen on old drawings and photographs of the local sites.

Thus, Warrington's glass industry reached its relative peak in the 1770s and 1780s and was then

The Orford Lane Glassworks c.1830 from a sketch by Robert Booth about the time of the retirement of its founder Thomas Kirkland Glazebrook. His works produced flint glass of the highest quality and Glazebrook was regarded as a leading figure in the Lancashire glass industry. The management of the works was taken over by Thomas Robinson and a new glassmaking dynasty established itself in Warrington.

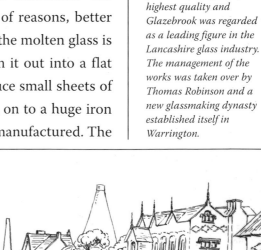

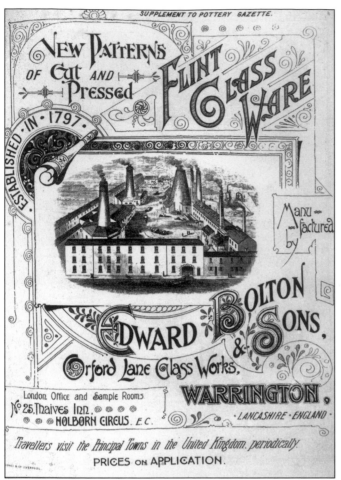

In 1855 Robinson's nephew took over the Orford Lane works and formed a new partnership with Edward Bolton. By 1869 Robinson decided to set himself up in a new works at Bank Quay, and the Orford Lane works continued to make Flint Glass under Bolton's control until 1892. The site was subsequently acquired by the new enterprise of the Alliance Box Works.

The earliest view of Robinson's Mersey Glassworks printed from an original paper negative of the late 1860s. The barrels on the quayside may have been landed for the adjacent Crosfield's soapworks. The original single cone of the new works can be seen in the background.

Although Robinson's may be Warrington's best-known maker of Warrington Glass, it was Perrin, Geddes & Co. which produced some of the finest. This superb cut-glass decanter was of a type commissioned by the Corporation of Liverpool on the occasion of a visit by the then Prince of Wales (later George IV.) To complement the elaborate banquet of delicacies from every season, the finest table glass was commissioned from Perin, Geddes & Co of Bank Quay. Surprisingly the gourmet Prince was more taken with the glassware than the feast and asked the mayor of Liverpool to order him a quantity of the glass from the same manufacturer. An initial order of 12 decanters, six dozen claret and port glasses, 36 coolers and six water jugs was thought to be too modest and further glassware was added. The Prince of Wales' service was naturally engraved with his Royal crest; took over a year to make and left Liverpool council with a bill of just over £1,300.

increasingly overshadowed by that of its neighbour. As late as 1851, 162 people were employed in the town's glassworks, and in 1891 almost 200 in the glassworks and in potterymaking, but by that time the industry in St Helens had over 4,000 workers. The surviving works in Warrington was Robinson's, on the northern side of the railway line at Factory Lane, Bank Quay. The firm's Mersey Flint Glass Works, rebuilt in the mid-19th century, survived until 1933, though the nearby Bank Quay Glassworks closed at the beginning of the century. Glass House Row, 19 tiny terraced houses without even a backyard, was an early example of purpose-built workers' housing, built directly alongside the Bank Quay glassworks yard in the mid-1830s. Glassmaking left little trace in Warrington and now few people recall that it was once a significant industry in the town. The fact that it did not flourish is essentially because of geographical accident. Had the coalfield extended a couple of miles further south it is possible that the industry would have grown much larger and rivalled that of St Helens – after all, Warrington was a pioneer in the early development of glassmaking in the region.

By the late 1890s the scale of the operation at the Mersey Glassworks had considerably expanded and there were now three glass cones with their furnaces in operation.

This view of Robinson's works shows its proximity to the Bank Quay railway line which may have proved a factor in Robinson's decision to relocate from Orford Lane.

By the early 20th century Robinson's glass cutters were threatened not only by the flood of cheaper press-moulded glass but also by foreign competition. In January 1912 a 'Dumping Exhibition' was staged at the Empire Skating Rink, as part of a political campaign to levy protective taxes on foreign imports. Robinson's products was prominently displayed and the Warrington Guardian *reported: 'Much attention will be focussed upon the glass stall which has been furnished with exhibits by the Mersey Flint Glass Co Ltd. The exhibits include glass ware made for the late King Edward, his son King George, The Duke of Westminster and many well-known aristocratic families. The glassware is contrasted with the manufacture of Germany and other countries.'*

A view inside Robinson's cutting shop in the late 19th century showing the enlarged scale of their operations. The cutting shop was not the healthiest of places to work because of the use of arsenic in the production process! By this time Robinson's had established a reputation for the production of fine cut glass tableware which was shipped worldwide. The works covered three acres of land and they employed about 180 workers. A cut-glass decanter would take a week to produce by the cutter alone.

In a last-ditch attempt to ensure the survival of the business, Robinson's land and buildings were sold to Crosfield's for the sum of £41,000 in 1918. By 1933 attempts to continue the operations were abandoned and many of the workers were transferred to Birmingham. The glassworks buildings were eventually demolished by Crosfield's who were redeveloping their operations and Warrington's last link with glassmaking had disappeared.

Soap

THE lower Mersey shores, from Liverpool up to Warrington, saw many early developments in the chemical and related industries, including soap, candles and dyes. This was developing as early as the 1750s but the major growth of the industry occurred after 1800, when soapmaking, in particular, experienced a considerable expansion. The production of soap was originally associated with other trades drawing their raw materials from agriculture, because it was made from rendered tallow (beef fat) which was boiled with salt and oils to precipitate the soap. Early soap smelled disagreeable and was of poor quality, but as Britain's colonial empire expanded the tallow was supplemented by imported palm and vegetable oils which were landed at Liverpool and brought upriver to Warrington. The salt was, of course, available in unlimited quantities in Cheshire, while the coal required for the boiling process was found just north of Warrington in the south Lancashire coalfield. The switch to oils did not mean that the tallow was no longer of value, for it was refined and became a major ingredient of commercially mass-produced candles.

Warrington's soap industry, later one of its most important trades, was started in 1814 when Joseph Crosfield opened his small works at Bank Quay. The Crosfields were a Kendal family and had no previous involvement with soap or chemicals, but they had Warrington connections and young Joseph was initially apprenticed to a grocer in the town. He left the grocery trade, but his experience of the business gave him an excellent working knowledge of commodities such as soap, and ways of marketing products. He bought a disused factory at Bank Quay (previously an iron

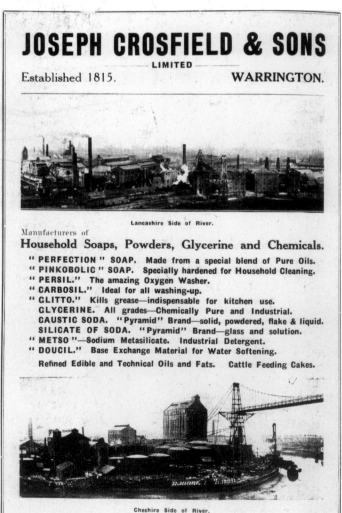

JOSEPH CROSFIELD & SONS
LIMITED
Established 1815.   WARRINGTON.

Lancashire Side of River.

Manufacturers of
Household Soaps, Powders, Glycerine and Chemicals.

"PERFECTION" SOAP. Made from a special blend of Pure Oils.
"PINKOBOLIC" SOAP. Specially hardened for Household Cleaning.
"PERSIL." The amazing Oxygen Washer.
"CARBOSIL." Ideal for all washing-up.
"CLITTO." Kills grease—indispensable for kitchen use.
GLYCERINE. All grades—Chemically Pure and Industrial.
CAUSTIC SODA. "Pyramid" Brand—solid, powdered, flake & liquid.
SILICATE OF SODA. "Pyramid" Brand—glass and solution.
"METSO"—Sodium Metasilicate. Industrial Detergent.
"DOUCIL." Base Exchange Material for Water Softening.
Refined Edible and Technical Oils and Fats.   Cattle Feeding Cakes.

Cheshire Side of River.

foundry and small wireworks) and in 1815 it began producing soap. The coal came from Haydock, salt from Northwich, the alkali, or lye, from the ash of kelp or seaweed, imported from Scotland and Ireland, tallow from local slaughter-houses and palm oil from the Americas via Liverpool. The works grew slowly, for at this time there was intense competition in the soapmaking industry and even in the late 1830s, when it was producing about 900 tons of soap a year, Crosfield's was only the 25th largest producer in England (out of 296 listed). In the 1850s and 1860s production became more sophisticated and scientific, while new materials were employed – notably, the replacement of lye with artificially made soda (sodium carbonate) produced by boiling salt with sulphuric acid, then roasting the resultant 'cake' of sodium sulphate with limestone and coal to make 'black ash' from which the soda was leached by soaking in water. This was known, after its inventor, as the Leblanc Process and it was the basis of the great Widnes chemical industry. Widnes, and other local chemical works, thus supplied a key material for the many soapworks in the area. Crosfield's eventually bought their soda from the chemical works owned by the Gamble family at St Helens.

By the early 1860s Crosfield's had become one of the top five manufacturers, and at this stage the decision was taken to buy up any available land which came on the market in the vicinity of Bank Quay, so there would be plenty of room for future expansion. The diversity of small factories in and around Bank Quay produced a piecemeal and fragmented land ownership, and it took over 25 years

Crosfield's Gold Medal soaps are packed for despatch, including their trademark Erasmic Herb toilet soap. By 1913 over 500 of the firm's 3,000 workforce were women and girls and they only took on school leavers of 14 and over, paying an extra 1s 0d a week to those who had better qualifications. Attendance at night school three times a week was compulsory where 'the course of instruction for boys is naturally concerned with questions relating to their special line of work. The girls are encouraged to take an interest in domestic economy, and are, in fact, required to learn needle-work, dressmaking, cookery, and laundry work...'. Crosfield's had thus ensured that all their female employees would make good housewives on their marriage, at which point they had to leave the firm.

This charming example of one of Crosfield's many advertising campaigns demonstrates their popular Perfection household and laundry soap, a boon to housewives everywhere.

Production of Crosfield's household soap began here as 'a mixture of purified oils and fats is boiled with a caustic soda solution in steam-heated pans holding anything from five to 100 tons of soap'.

for Crosfield's to acquire all the land which they needed (including property on the south bank of the river). When, in the mid-1880s, the Bolton grocer William Lever was seeking a site for his soapworks he came to Bank Quay, perhaps to compete with the old-established firm of Crosfield's on its home ground, and it was here that the first Sunlight soap was manufactured in 1885. Lever, though, recognised that there was insufficient land for future growth and, as he was deeply interested in town and country planning, housing issues, economic efficiency and large-scale rational industrial development, he founded instead the utopian new community of Port Sunlight built around its model factory. Shrewdly, though, he retained the Warrington factory. Crosfield's continue to update their own technology – in 1883 the Warrington factory was lit by electricity, one of the first such industrial plants in the world – but by 1910 the firm had apparently reached the limit of its growth. In a fiercely competitive trade, and with the innovative and dynamic William Lever as its arch-rival just down the river, Crosfield's was unable to expand its market share. It pioneered the development of soap powders and in 1909 Persil, perhaps the world's best-known soap powder, was first produced here, but the firm simply could not survive alone and in 1919 it was taken over by its upstart junior rival, Lever Brothers. The production of soap in the town flourished, however, and it became for many people a symbol of Warrington itself because of the highly-visible location of the main Bank Quay

works, immediately alongside the West Coast railway line.

Soapmaking was a relatively small employer throughout the 19th century, because output remained modest by later standards. Historians have commented that the great increase in the use of soap in the last quarter of the 19th century was a social change with enormous implications. The cost of raw materials declined steadily (for example, steamships meant that palm oil could be imported from the colonies in much greater quantities and more cheaply) and this meant that in real terms the retail price of soap fell sharply after 1870. Many more families could afford to buy it. Public health improvements had a major impact, as did the realisation among medical experts that a simple application of soap and water could make a huge difference to personal and domestic hygiene and therefore to the incidence and spread of infectious diseases. Late

Victorian notions of cleanliness being 'next to godliness' were a very significant factor in promoting the use of soap. Most ordinary families could now afford soap because the price was lower; they could use soap because they had piped water; and they knew about the value of soap because their children were told about cleanliness at school, and the newspapers were beginning to advertise and promote its use for washing self, clothes and house. Demand rose extremely quickly and the industry innovated and expanded.

Soap was made by hand at Crosfield's for most of the 19th century. The great vats in which the raw ingredients were melted together and boiled with strong brine or soda were stirred by hand using great wooden paddles; the liquid soap was scooped out and poured off in buckets, which had to be carried manually from room to room; any perfumes or colourings were stirred in using long wooden spoons; and the blocks of set soap were cut by hand using long wires (rather like an old-fashioned cheese-cutter) to give square bars which were wrapped and labelled by women workers. Even in 1891 only 88 people in the town were employed in the industry, but the number of workers rose rapidly in the 1920s and 1930s in line with fast-growing output of soap powders and quality soaps. The firm was notable in many ways. It employed a high proportion of women, especially in the packaging and labelling departments. The Crosfield family had very strong liberal attitudes, and were equally strong Liberals politically. They held a progressive view of how a workforce should be treated, and thus Crosfields offered a range of benefits far ahead of most other firms – health

The production of toilet soap involved further stages of production to produce a soap suitable for delicate complexions. Contemporary company brochures explain the process: 'The purest soap obtainable, made from selected materials, is reduced to shreds and dried in hot air stoves. The shreds are passed several times between the massive granite rollers [seen here] ...to make it thoroughly smooth, and to allow of the perfume and colour being mixed in a cold state. The soap, saturated with scent, is now in ribbons, and is ready to enter into a machine called The Plodder ("La Peloteuse"). This machine by means of an Archimedean screw squeezes the shreds of soap into one homogeneous whole, delivering it in the form of one continuous bar. The bar is cut and shaped into tablets.'

protection and sickness pay, communal facilities and organisations (including its own Girl Guide company and choir), and 'rewards' such as outings and social events. In this, and in their much greater care for the physical conditions of work, Crosfield's was the most advanced and enlightened employer in the town, and its worker loyalty was correspondingly high. Whether this policy encouraged their workers to support family members as parliamentary candidates for Warrington is not clear. For much of the late 19th and early 20th century the town was represented by the great political enemies of the Crosfields, the strongly Conservative Greenall brewing dynasty – but they had the inestimable advantage of the formidable and tireless Lady Greenall, the Conservatives' not-so-secret weapon in the years before World War One.

The production of soap was becoming a more scientific process and, to keep ahead of their competitors, Crosfield employed 'a large staff of chemists, whose specialised university training has qualified them for enthusiastic research and experimental work in the laboratories'.

Here Crosfield's household soap is being stamped into tablets by the machinery which could produce over 34 tons a day by 1913. Crosfield's considered themselves to be caring employers but working conditions could be less pleasant in the departments producing their brands of household cleaners, as Mrs Shawcross – who worked there in the 1920s – recalls: "Crosfield's was the best place in town to work. If you worked at Crosfield's you'd got a good job. They were a bit strict. I worked in the Carbosil – which was used for washing up. The Carbosil was floating about that much that we used to wear a handkerchief round our faces. It didn't do your chest any good. The Carbosil finished so we got transferred to Persil, making packets. I wasn't in a union, not in them days."

In this view of the light and airy Tablet Room the workers are putting the finishing touches to the toilet soap.

Elsewhere in the factory these young workers are at work on Crosfield's packaging.

Behind the scenes the work of refining chemicals was carried out. These were needed, not only for Crosfield's own products, but were sold on for a variety of industrial processes. Eventually these two areas of Crosfield's production would emerge as virtually separate firms sharing the Bank Quay site.

Crosfield's had a fleet of Thornycroft lorries to delivery Persil, Glitto scouring powder and the famous Pinkobolic soap on daily journeys within a 60-mile radius and to customers far and wide.

One of Crosfield's best-known products, Persil washing powder, revolutionised washing day. Gone were the days of rubbing and scrubbing, Persil
cleaned clothes 'by virtue of liberating free oxygen' during the boiling and
rinsing process. As dolly tub and posser gave way to electric washing
machines Persil continued to evolve to be a market-leading product.

This was one of the scenes which greeted King George V and Queen
Mary on their visit to the works in July 1913 when they saw the
latest production methods and machinery in use.

By the 1960s further innovations had been introduced on the Surf production line, and Crosfield's had long been part of the Unilever Group.
Rationalisation would soon move Surf manufacture to Port Sunlight
leaving Persil as the major product of Warrington's Lever Bros' plant
whilst Crosfield's now concentrated on chemical production rather than
their trademark soaps.

In 1915 Arthur Crosfield, head of the family firm and former Liberal MP for
Warrington was knighted. Crosfield's had given him the finances to sustain
the role of an international playboy in his youth. In 1907 he married the
daughter of a Greek merchant and by 1910 the couple were major players in
London's social scene. The mundane activities of soap manufacture palled and he sold out to the firm's old rival at Port Sunlight. Sir Arthur and
Lady Crosfield now entertained royalty at Witanhurst, their magnificent new mansion high on Hampstead Heath. More recently it has achieved a
new notoriety as the location of BBC television's Fame Academy!

A Package Deal

THE production of board and paper was not one of Warrington's traditional industries and during the 19th century it was a very minor element in the town's diverse economic structure. Papermaking was an industry associated with north-west England in the 18th and 19th centuries but the great majority of papermills were located in the Darwen, Rossendale and Bury area. However, the demand for paper and cardboard grew very rapidly indeed during the second half of the century. By 1900 England was a fully-literate nation as a result of the introduction of compulsory education 30 years earlier. This had generated a massive new demand for reading matter (including cheap fiction, popular editions of novels and literary works, and the advent of mass circulation national and regional newspapers). England was becoming a more bureaucratic country and 'the paperwork' was growing – typewriters and the earliest forms of multiple copying meant that the use of paper in offices grew as a result.

This interior view of the Alliance Boxworks was taken before the fire of 1919 which destroyed the premises which the company had taken over from Robinson's glassworks in Orford Lane. The male foreman wears a 'Billy-cock' hat as a sign of his authority over the female operatives who are bending and slotting sheets of chipboard or strawboard to make boxes and lids.

In addition, as the consumer age was well under way, more and more paper and card were needed for packaging and presentation of goods sold in the shops. Of course the 20th century saw this process reach hitherto undreamed of levels of extravagance, and packaging became an obsession, but the signs were very clear even in the years before 1900. The consequence was that the paper-making industry moved away from its traditional locations and new factories were established in areas where consumer industries were situated. This shift was taking place by 1900 but became very noticeable in the 1920s and 1930s and a report on the regional economy written in the early 1960s emphasised that 'recent growth [in papermaking] has been quickest in the Warrington district'.

In the early 1900s two men saw Warrington's potential a location for the packaging industry. In his newly acquired premises in Orford Lane Felix Maginn set up a single-room factory with second-hand machinery and a staff of eight – the Alliance Box Works was born. Despite some initial setbacks Maginn secured contracts to supply local firms including the soap industry. By the time of the founder's death in the mid 1920s the firm had expanded to occupy the former premises of a velvet cutting works and the site of the Orford Lane glassworks. More crucially Maginn had also acquired business acumen and up-to-date machinery from the United States and spread his empire to Partington, where the company's new mills supplied boxboard for conversion into containers at the Warrington plant. Meanwhile Thomas Chadwick brought his papermaking firm from Oldham, acquiring the Howley Mill and converting it to paper production.

In 1937 a much larger firm, Thames Board, opened its new Mersey works at Warrington to serve as a northern production centre for cardboard, packaging materials and cartons. Here we can see, very clearly illustrated, the value of Warrington's excellent location. Although this was two decades before the construction of the motorway network, the plans for a national highway system were already being formulated and it was obvious that Warrington would be a major interchange in the future. It was of course already well situated on the railway network, and it was equidistant between the Manchester and Merseyside conurbations, where demand for the packaging products was high. Geographical position, rather than an established tradition of paper and card production, was

This Alliance Box adver-tisement of 1948 features some of their typical products and shows the three works sites off Orford Lane.

This view of Norman
Street shows the three
main sites of the Alliance
Box Company. Offices and
production were combined
in the concrete building in
the background on Orford
Lane which replaced the
earliest premises destroyed
by the fire of 1919. To the
right is the East Works
containing the Corrugator
which produced corru-
gated fibreboard. On the
left is the West Works, (the
only surviving building)
which was started in 1937.
East and West Works were
linked by a bridge which
disguised a conveyor belt
to move complete and
part-processed board.
Waiting patiently in the
delivery bay in the West
Works are two horses
which have probably just
ferried a heavy load of
large reels of paper or flat
strawboard from a barge
on the River Mersey at
Howley Quay. Meanwhile
the sheeted vehicle at the
bottom of Norman Street
has just delivered reels of
paper to be used in the
manufacture of the corru-
gated fibreboard. On the
right a large lorry is poised
to take a large load of
paper board waste away
for recycling.

instrumental in the decision to locate the new factory at Warrington. The new complex was built on very modern lines, with a technologically-advanced production process. The factory was an early leader in the field of recycling, taking in waste paper from much of north-west England and processing it to make cardboard and cheap packing materials. Long after the mills have closed Thames Board may be best remembered in local history as the site of the town's only major air raid of World War Two, on 14 September 1940, when a single bomb, dropped on the autumn fete, being held in the grounds, killed 16 people and badly injured many others.

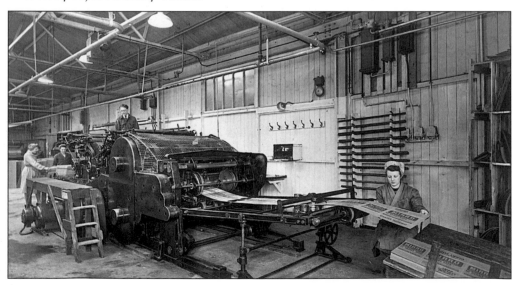

Ernest Davenport stands
guard on the footboard of
a two-colour rotary printer
bending machine during
the production of cases for
Mirro scouring powder.
This photograph was taken
inside the wooden section
of the concrete building in
Orford Lane.

Frank McKie describes the scene in the machine room which ran the whole length of the East Works and housed the Corrugator: "In the foreground the corrugated board is being taken off the machine after it has been manufactured to the correct size. The Corrugator was able to reproduce a continuous sheet of double-faced board which could be slit and chopped to the required size of any corrugated case blank. At the far end of the Corrugator 63 foot wide paper reels were positioned on the machine and fed through the corrugating and combining process. The fibreboard was then conveyed to the adjoining processing area where the fibreboard cases were completely manufactured. The industry has made great advances since this photograph was taken in the late 1940s. Then the machine was running at a speed of approximately150 feet per minute; today's equivalent would be 500-600 foot per minute."

Until the 1950s the Alliance Box Company manufactured fancy or plain covered boxes. Here paper is being applied by hand after being coated with an adhesive. Although this seems a routine task it took experience to know the drying time of the adhesive and to recognise the various types of boxes and paper in use.

The Alliance Box Company made Wood Frame End containers for a number of customer including Jacob's Biscuits of Liverpool. Frank McKie recalls the manufacturing process which is seen here (below) in 1950: "The ends of the container consisted of a wooden frame made with mitred corners which were wire stitched together. A sheet of solid fibreboard was then wire stitched to this frame. Here the bales of frame ends are tied together ready for despatch. The customer would then make up the container by positioning a four-panel pre-bent solid board sheet around the two end frames and nailing or stitching this box body to the outside of the wooden frames. Alternatively the box body could also have been joined along its length by wire stitching. This made a container which just needed the wood frame ends inserting and securing at either end. The whole container was manufactured on site at Alliance Box and would probably also be printed on the panels with all the information required by the customer. These containers were used for anything for engineering parts to the biscuits but production ceased later in the 1950s due to a decline in demand."

PAPER BAG MAKERS
and PRINTERS to the
PAPER TRADE

HOWLEY PAPER WORKS

Joseph Chadwick & Sons .. Ltd.
Howley Paper Works
WARRINGTON

Chadwick's paperworks at Howley, seen here in a trade advert of 1934, expanded over it's 25 years on the site as the Warrington Examiner *newspaper reported in 1933: 'Today the works at Howley cover almost three acres of land, have a third of a mile roadway through them, house some 150 highly-specialised machines, and can turn out in one week more than 30 million paper bags – [in total] weighing more than 100 tons. For those whose imagination is caught by these marvels of mechanism at Howley Paperworks, one could write much of these machines which stamp, cut, paste and print – in two colours if necessary – paper bags at the rate of 300 or 400 a minute.'*

In 1936 Thames Board Mills (seen above) expanded their operation from Purfleet in Essex by opening its huge purpose built factory at Arpley and creating almost 300 new jobs locally. The Warrington Examiner *described the scale of their operations: "Hundreds of tons of raw material such as wood-pulp and waste paper arrive by barge and lorry, to be picked up by gantry cranes and run into the huge storage sheds. Then the raw materials proceed directly to the first process of manufacturing. The whole mill is thus a model of industrial planning and secures a direct flow-through from raw materials to the finished product."*

Inside the mill the latest machinery was installed and the Examiner *again waxed lyrical about it:.' The new machines at Warrington run at higher speeds than have previously been secured on plant of their type. The entire mill is marked by the latest technical features.' Increased speed of machinery and the sheer scale of the operations brought increased risk of injury. Thames Board Mills was proud of its health and safety record and its personnel relations.*

A brief respite from churning out paper bags for these Chadwick's workers as they pose resignedly for the camera. Meanwhile managing director Mr Fred. Chadwick was in upbeat mood about this company: "We have been building up steadily, and increasing business by the introduction of new products and machinery, and today we have reason to believe that our business is still increasing."

Many of Chadwick's workers in the 1920s and 30s were recruited from the surrounding Howley area, beginning work at the age of 14 with a day that lasted from 7.30am until 5.30pm. Looking back on their experiences 50 years later, members of the Howley Memories Group recalled only the bad old days. One teenager was less than impressed with a sizable pay rise: "By God, I'd worked for it! By the time you got your 2s [10p] they'd put your speed up and you was working twice as much for the same money." Another member summed up her feelings with the comment: "I don't know whether I was more happy at leaving than getting married!"

Retailing

A GOOD deal of the earlier part of this book considers industries and looks at the working conditions and experiences of people in factories, mills, and workshops, but this was never the whole story. There was a lot more to Warrington than industry, and the prosperity of the town for 1,000 years has depended heavily upon retailing and commerce. We know that there were shops (that is, permanent premises in the main streets, rather than stalls in the market) in Warrington by the late 16th century. The history of the market itself can be traced back with certainty to the 13th century, a continuous record stretching over 700 years, but there is no doubt that there has been some sort of market in the town for nearly 1,000 years. Shops were a later development, but the modern centre, based on the four streets meeting at Market Gate, was taking shape over 400 years ago. Warrington's grocers and drapers, butchers and greengrocers, were an elite within the town. They were among the wealthiest citizens and lived 'over the shop' in the most prestigious addresses – Bridge Street, Horsemarket Street and Buttermarket Street. It was not until the middle of the 18th century that wealthier people began to favour edge of town residences. The records of these shopkeepers tell us of the considerable comfort in which they lived, and also give information about the very wide range of goods available for the townspeople to buy if they had the money three centuries ago. We find references to exotic spices, silk, tobacco and brandy; consumer goods such as painted pottery, clocks, playing cards, framed engravings and embroidered hangings; and a huge variety of 'every-day' items, from ink and paper and quills, through nails and locks, combs and shoelaces, to lace trimmings for gowns, spectacles for the short-sighted, children's alphabet books, and turpentine.

Retailers began to specialise and advertise. The earliest street directories, published in the years around 1800, give valuable information about the leading businesses of the time, but by the late 19th century we have many more advertisements published in newspapers and local journals. The market continued to flourish and in the 1850s was extensively remodelled with a new covered market hall: it could accommodate more traders but was also more orderly, tidy and better-managed. The old ramshackle market buildings and court house were swept away and traders were forbidden to set up stalls in the nearby streets –

Bridge Street had been Warrington's main shopping street from medieval times, profiting from the travellers crossing Warrington's Bridge especially on market days. By the time of this remarkable photograph of the mid-1850s it was a mixture of centuries-old small timber-framed buildings and their newer brick-built neighbours, reflecting Warrington's growing prosperity by the early 19th century. The three old shops on the immediate right of this picture were shortly to be replaced by the premises later occupied by Hancock and Wood, one of the last family-run stores still flourishing in Warrington's 21st-century shopping centre.

Sankey Street, which was particularly narrow, had frequently been almost impassable because of obstructions on market days. By the end of the 19th century, therefore, Warrington had become one of the leading commercial and retailing centres in the north-west, its catchment area extending north towards Newton, Burtonwood and Culcheth and south into rural Cheshire.

The importance of retailing as an employer is demonstrated by the 1891 census, which showed almost 1,500 people engaged in 'selling' of one sort or another (roughly three-quarters of these were in the 'food dealing' sector, including the town centre groceries and greengroceries, the market stalls, and many small corner shops). The retailing trades accounted for about 12 per cent of the town's workforce, and a substantial proportion of female workers. Many of the people recorded by the census were employees. They did not own shops, or manage them, but worked as shop assistants and servants. Their faces look out at us from contemporary images, for it was common for a shop to be photographed if it had, for example, a particularly fine window display. Especially popular were the displays put on for Christmas, when hams, poultry and other delicacies would be hung in decorative fashion in front of the shop, often wreathed in garlands. The shops competed to provide the most elaborate and mouthwatering display, and all the staff, from smallest shopboy to oldest retainer, would stand outside in formal poses with starched white aprons and best coats.

Life for shop assistants was not easy. Opening hours were very long by the standards of the 1950s and 1960s (though nowadays, with greater freedom in hours and times, the opening hours of shops are again lengthening). The conditions of work were often difficult. Assistants came early, did a lot of manual labour, had few breaks, and left late. Nonetheless, working in a shop (at least, a respectable town centre emporium with customers of quality) was deemed to give considerable status to a young man or woman. Such work was cleaner, less hazardous and for most people more agreeable than being in heavy industry or domestic service. It may have been tiring, the pay many not have been princely, but it was 'nice'. In most shops the assistants were expected to wear a uniform, the girls with spotless white aprons or overalls, the boys with shining shoes and neatly-pressed trousers. That, too, set them apart from, and a bit higher than, manual workers and domestics. Larger shops also employed a whole host of other staff, who did not wait and serve and attend the customers but were doing other tasks – armies of delivery boys whizzed around the town on

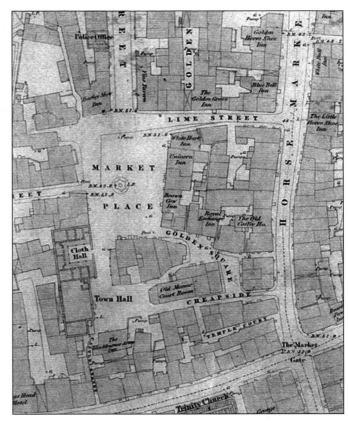

bicycles and brought anything from sausages to shoes and socks to the customer's home (especially if the customer lived in a respectable road or a new development of villas). In the backyard behind the shop men heaved and shifted the boxes of goods on and off wagons or worked in the stores packing and unpacking. There were the cashiers and account-keepers (for ladies did not pay in cash, ever – they had their own personal account and discreetly, at intervals, they paid off the outstanding bills). There were the women who polished the mahogany counters, brass fittings, new gleaming plate glass windows, and tiled floors.

In retrospect, the years around 1900 were the golden age for the traditional family-run firm. The owners, often in the business for several generations, enjoyed high status in the community and an established place in local society. They were leading figures in the town, often serving on the council, meeting at the Chamber of Trade, paying for splendid advertisements in directories and yearbooks, competing to introduce a new line or an eyecatching display. Though they might rival each other, collectively they were unchallenged in the town. But danger signals were apparent by 1910. The multiple stores were appearing and regional and national chains were extending their tentacles. They opened shops which offered more than even the most dynamic locally-owned firm – many additional lines, very sophisticated marketing ploys, loss-leaders, special offers and, with their superior spending power, the ability to buy up or rent key central area sites. Woolworth's, Boots, and Marks and Spencer's, for example, all grew on the strength of the chain formula so that by 1930 hardly a town of any size or significance was without at least one branch of these. In the case of Warrington, Boots had two stores by 1908, and multiple grocers such as Home & Colonial

Warrington's market was originally located at the crossroads of Market Gate but, by the time of this Ordnance Survey map of 1851, pressure of traffic had forced it to move to the area which is now known as Golden Square shopping centre. Numerous inns, including the Barley Mow, served the weary traders and customers, and the butcher's quarter was to be found in Cheapside. As the needs of shoppers changed the site was redeveloped in the mid-1850s to create a new indoor Market Hall and again in the 1980s to provide a modern shopping mall.

The redevelopment of Warrington Market Place in the mid-1850s had included the building of a covered 'shed' attached to the new Market Hall. The cast iron shed became the centre for the fishmongers, and dairy produce. In this photograph taken shortly before the closure of the Old Fishmarket in 1974, Mottershead's offer eggs and cheese on the left whilst wholesome tripe can be bought on the immediate right. The Barley Mow Inn can be seen in the background with the old General Market located to its rear.

Stores and Lipton's also had branches in the town by then, while Woolworth's came to Sankey Street in 1913.

During the mid-20th century family-run firms found the world ever more competitive. It was not simply that they were unable to take advantage of economies of scale, bulk-buying and other strategies pursued by the multiples. The multiples had an air of modernity and fashionable appeal which old-established small shops could not easily challenge. Some local firms, notably Hancock & Wood, adapted and introduced the principle of the department store, but by the 1950s many others were finding it hard to survive. The pressure for town centre redevelopment exacerbated their difficulties. Family firms saw their premises purchased for redevelopment but were unable to afford the rents in the shopping centres which replaced them. In Warrington the crisis time for many local firms was the late 1960s, when these trends came together with the beginning of the redevelopment of almost the entire central area. Today very few of the names familiar from 40 years ago remain. The shops in Golden Square are almost all multiples and nationally-known chains.

In Warrington, too, another dramatic change of the late 20th century had a tremendous impact. This was one of the first towns in England where out-of-town retail parks were built. The new town plan of the late 1960s assumed that shopping would continue to be focussed on the old town centre, but by the time development was under way in the mid-1970s there was very strong commercial pressure for retail parks on the edge, close to motorway links and accessible only

By the late 1880s a new General Market had been built further down in Market Street, behind the Barley Mow and its distinctive gabled-roofline can be seen in the centre left of this picture. The whole market place became the focal point for the sale of fresh produce although, even in the early 20th century, shop keepers had no refrigerators to preserve perishable stock. This could work to the advantage of the poorest families as Harry Hardman recalls: "After the 1914-18 War a mighty lot of women couldn't afford to go shopping at the weekend until 8 or 9 o'clock at night. There was no refrigeration so all the traders either had to throw the stuff away or get rid of it, so the incentive was to get what they could for it. The women had to feed their families and you'd see them turning out from all points of the compass and converging in on Market Gate and the Old Market. You'd see butchers having an auction inside their own shop – 'Who'll give me half a crown, two bob for this?' Then the women would move around to the fish or vegetable market. You rarely saw fresh fruit because most people couldn't afford it but you could afford 'faded' apples and 'faded' oranges because they were really at a give away price."

by road. The great Gemini complex was slotted into the earlier plan, revolutionising Warrington's retail role in the region but also tilting the balance of shopping within the borough. It reinforced the status of Warrington as one of the most important shopping centres in the north-west, but it challenged the supremacy of its town centre. The threat to the centre forced the borough council to implement major improvements in order to maintain its attractions and commercial viability. This, thankfully, has been a largely successful policy and today the town centre thrives, but it could easily have been otherwise. Retailing (with related activities such as hotels and restaurants) now accounts for about a quarter of all employment in the borough, the highest proportion ever. The staff of IKEA and Marks and Spencer at Gemini are as much a part of Warrington's history as the delivery boys in grocery stores 100 years ago or the women who sold vegetables on the market in the reign of Elizabeth I.

*Fresh conger eel, skate,
halibut, plaice and haddock
are just some of the produce
to be had from this female
fishmonger in the years
before World War One.*

*Improvements would soon be on the way for Reardon's fish stall as the old wooden stalls were due for a makeover in 1913, but for practical rather
than cosmetic reasons. 'The new stalls will consist of marble slates resting on iron legs, and, while this will keep the fish fresh and cool, the stalls will
be practically rat proof.'*

Charlie Lee's stall was a well-known feature of Warrington Fish Market in the 1950s because of the daily poem which was penned by its owner (seen just to the right of his stall). Writing in the Warrington Guardian *in 1969 Dr Johnson Ball recalled: 'In the corner near the Barley Mow was Charlie Lee's oyster stall. When he was ready for business Charlie hung a glass case containing a crab's claw which appeared to be the exact shape of a human leg. He also wrote poem which he put up for people to read. He was quite a character and though in our innocence we were a little afraid of his pock-marked countenance, there was nothing to fear.'*

A splendid array of Christmas turkeys awaited customers of Bowcock's market stall before the days of deep-frozen or sanitised plastic wrapped birds on polystyrene trays.

Apart from hygiene considerations there were other hazards attached to open displays of food. In 1906 the police finally solved a series of baffling 'ham liftings' from the tempting display outside Price's Store in Buttermarket Street. With the aid of a piece of string tied to a ham they trapped the daring thief- who was astonished to find her prize was suddenly whisked away from concealment under her cloak by the watching constable.

Taylor's grocery store in Buttermarket Street had a typical shop window display of neat piles of tins, packets and colourful adverts to tempt the customers inside.

In the days before pre-packed goods unscrupulous traders might cheat their customers by giving short-weight. Warrington Borough Council's weights and measures inspectors undertake one of their periodic checks in the 1950s, watched by the anxious shop assistant.

The staff of Milling's grocery store stand poised to serve their customers. Until the days of the supermarket Milling's operated a popular local family chain of high-class stores in Warrington. Stan Smith recalls his experiences there before World War Two: "After about six months working in the warehouse of Millings I wanted a change so I asked if I could go into the shop to learn how to serve on the counter. I was given the chance and had to wear a white coat and white apron. I went on the counter to learn how to serve bacon, ham, cheese and eggs plus other groceries. I really enjoyed this and was soon cutting bacon and had a space on the counter. From then on I used to have my regular customers who came to me. When I was about 17½ years old, my boss at Milling's Warrington shop asked me to go to the branch shop in Latchford. The manager there had taken ill and the assistant manager had to take charge. This meant that they needed another assistant to take over on the bacon, cheese and ham counter. This was a promotion for me and I felt that I was making something of my life.".

The manager, grocer's assistant and errand lad pose outside Melia's family grocery chain early in the 20th century.

Open all hours, the Orford Lane branch of Melia's store where the errand lad stands ready to deliver the customer's order on his hand cart.

Harding's family baker's shop in Dudley Street off Orford Lane is pictured here in the early 20th century.

Fresh bread was still delivered daily to customers in the 1950s, although motorised vehicles were gradually replacing the horse-drawn van. Ron Mottram remembers his days as a Co-operative Society breadman in the late 1950s: "I was 14 when I started at the Co-op as a van lad taking the bread out. In those days nearly everybody you went to you just left the bread and they paid you at weekends. I spent most of my time on a motorised bread van with a man named England. We used to go round Penketh and Sankey. One day we did Penketh and the next day we'd do Sankey. There were two lads, me and a lad named Fred Backhouse. You were out until all hours at night. Of course you didn't get any more money, you still only got you 11s 8d [less than 60p]. It was all part of the job but the work you did you seemed to enjoy. It was a bit like a social life as well as working. You got to know everybody and everybody got to know you."

As Warrington Corporation began to build large housing estates around the town there was a gradual realisation that they also needed to include the modern equivalent of corner shops. Gordon Hill remembers the family shop on the Loushers Lane estate in the late 1930s where the occupier needed to be more than just a shopkeeper: "The post office section took up one side, newspapers, sweets and sundries the other. There was a small lending library in the middle section. Dad was never in the best of health but would go out of his way to help in any way possible, helping people to fill in forms. Even when the shop was closed people would come knocking on the back door for various purchases, especially medicines like Glycerine, Lemon and Ipec, or Fennings Fever Cure."

Sankey Street was home to some of the town's major shops from the mid-19th century. These fine Gothic-style premises, built in 1864, were the purpose-built display rooms of Robert Garnett's and Sons, 'Cabinet Manufacturers, Decorators and Upholsterers'. Most of their ornately-carved furniture was produced on site in the workshops behind the premises and found its way into the houses of Warrington's new aristocracy of wealthy business men and the professional classes.

Woolworth's stores moved into Garnett's premises in 1913, targeting a completely different market, by selling 'Nothing over sixpence' [a mere 2½p]. Amongst the huge range of goods on offer were 'embroideries, millinery goods, drapery, fancy goods, veiling, gas goods and celluloid goods', as well as today's more recognisable stock of toys, sweets, stationery, music, china and cutlery.

DUTTON'S
—*the modern store*

Where Quality Goods for every Dress and Fashion need are displayed for your selection and satisfaction. ¶ *It is well to remember that mere cheapness in* DRESS WEAR *is more than offset by the conscious feeling that it looks cheap when worn.* ¶ DUTTON'S *never sacrifice quality for cheapness. This has been the policy for over one hundred years. Buy* DUTTON'S *Fashionable Wear in* COSTUMES, COATS, DRESSES *and* MILLINERY, *and feel well dressed——it's well worth while and worth more.* ¶ *The same principle applies to all our Departments——*FURNISHINGS, LINENS, FURNITURE, CARPETS *and* RUGS, CHINA, *etc.* ¶ *Quality Goods at Reasonable Prices.* ¶ *Comfortable Shopping facilities and Lifts to all Floors.*

'phone
519

J. & W. DUTTON L™.
DRAPERS AND FURNISHERS,
Sankey Street, Warrington.

Dutton's describes itself as 'the modern store' in this advertisement of 1934

**ARE OFFERING FOR AUTUMN WEAR
SPECIAL VALUE IN**
Ladies' & Maids' Coats

Coat as Sketch.
89/11
All Wool Velour.
Fur Trimmed.

We
give
Best
Value
and
Service.

Coat as Sketch.
95/11
All Wool Velour.
Very Smart Colours

BROADBENT & TURNER,
50/52, SANKEY ST., WARRINGTON.

By 1926 Broadbent & Turner were another old-established Warrington drapery firm in Warrington town centre.

Sir Peter Peacock, mayor of Warrington 1913-19, was the founder of a Warrington-based company which has ultimately become a national chain of stores. Like contemporary rivals Marks & Spencer, Peacock's empire seems to have begun on market stalls in and around Warrington, graduating to small shops on the outskirts of the town before reaching many high streets. When Sir Peter Peacock died in July 1948, his obituary-writer declared: 'He founded Peacock's Stores Ltd, opening branches in many parts of the country'. Mourners included representatives of Peacock's stores in Birmingham, West Bromwich, Gloucester, Widnes and Warrington. Today Peacock's are regarded as one of the up-and-coming businesses of the fashion world, a far cry from the company's original Penny Bazaar in Lyme Street.

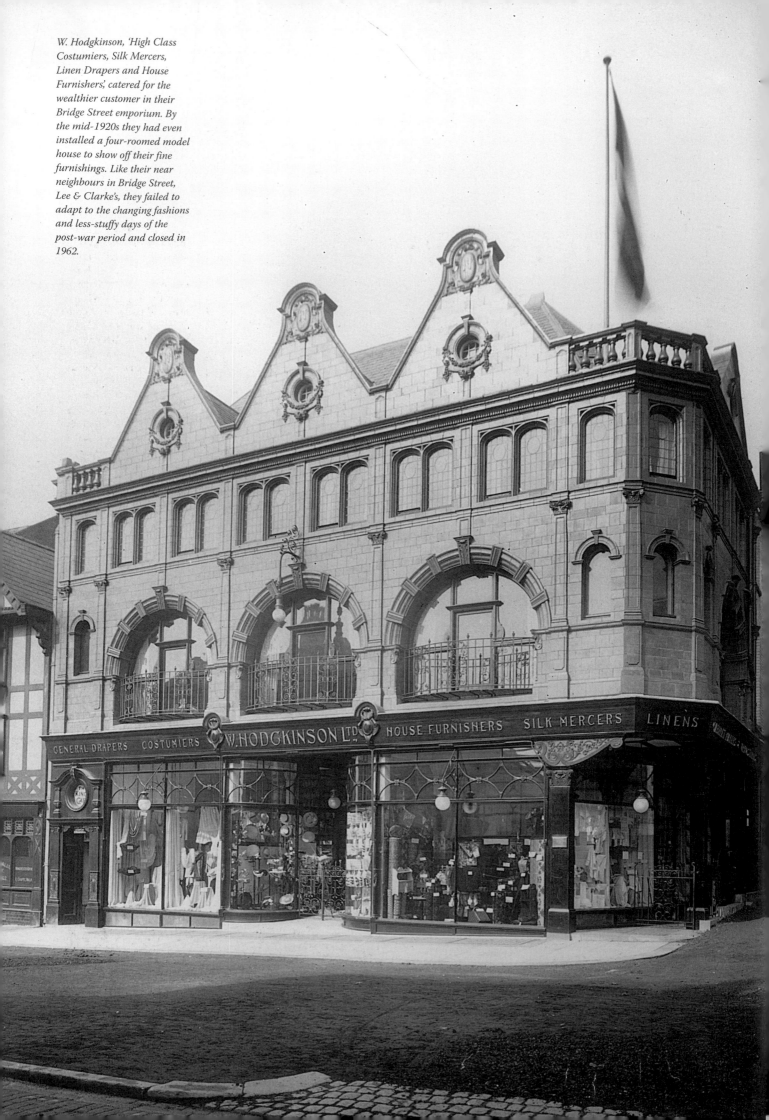

W. Hodgkinson, 'High Class Costumiers, Silk Mercers, Linen Drapers and House Furnishers', catered for the wealthier customer in their Bridge Street emporium. By the mid-1920s they had even installed a four-roomed model house to show off their fine furnishings. Like their near neighbours in Bridge Street, Lee & Clarke's, they failed to adapt to the changing fashions and less-stuffy days of the post-war period and closed in 1962.

The Professions

DURING the 20th century the word 'profession' became more widely applied than it was in the past. Several groups of workers now consider themselves 'professionals' wheras a century ago they would not have been regarded as such. Thus, teaching is now unquestionably a profession, but that was not so in the late Victorian period. A hundred years before that, doctors and medical men were rarely regarded as professionals. The only consistent element has been the legal world and the Church – for several hundred years lawyers have been professionals and, with the clergy of all ranks except perhaps the humble downtrodden curate, they were, into the 20th century, the elite in most towns.

One of the most important trends in employment is that society has placed an increasing value and status upon, for example, teachers, doctors, other health workers, and administrators in local government, who have achieved a higher status and – though many would claim otherwise in very recent times – a better rate of remuneration. In recent decades, for teachers, civil servants, lower ranks in the health service and some other groups, the upward trend has ended and others have overtaken them. New professions have emerged – management consultants, advertising and marketing executives, accountants (hardly regarded 100 years ago – they were mere servants of the company, who added up and subtracted the figures in the books). Such groups have carved niches for themselves, made themselves indispensable, and joined the ranks of the professionals. In the late 19th century they were a relatively small group, an elite which in Warrington as in many other places had a self-contained existence, with a separate social life, clubs and organisations, and its own power in

The Reverend Horace Powys, Rector of Warrington in the early 19th century, represented a traditional route into the professions. It had long been customary for junior members of the landed gentry to enter the priesthood whilst their older brothers either inherited the family title or made a military career. As owner of the former estates of the Boteler family, once Lords of the Manor of Warrington, Lord Lilford, his aristocratic relation, still had some influence over the living of the Parish Church. Reverend Powys is best remembered in Warrington for his connection with the town's annual Walking Day which he is rumoured to have started as a counter-attraction to Newton races.

The Reverend William Quekett, (seen here with his ambitious wife,) succeeded Powys as rector in the mid-1850s. He had progressed in the Church of England by his efforts amongst the poor in the East End of London. Although Warrington was one of the richest livings in the country he was unimpressed by the poverty he found in the town and the dilapidated state of the parish Church itself. In an effort to improve the expectations of his parishioners he organised an epic rail excursion of the towns-people to the revived Crystal Palace exhibition in London and raised funds for the rebuilding of the church.

Quekett's rebuilding of the Parish Church in the late 1850s found employment for the new profession of architect as well as the traditional craft of stone-mason. The church's crowning glory was its steeple which Quekett had financed by fundraising amongst his wealthier parishioners with the slogan, 'A guinea for a golden cock'.

behind-the-scenes activity, influencing and shaping decisions and policies. Today the professions are more numerous, more public, and less self-contained. They are no less influential, but they share their roles and influence with other groups in the town as a result of the increasing emphasis on democratic processes and openness.

We can trace the legal profession in Warrington into the 17th century, when the town was already a place to which people would come from surrounding villages if they needed the help of a lawyer. Two centuries later the town's lawyers were an important element in local society and played a key role in administration. For example, lawyers were prominent in the campaign by which the town achieved borough status in 1847.

It is no coincidence that the leader of the campaign, and the first mayor of the new borough of Warrington, was William Beamont, the town's top solicitor. At the same time the medical profession was evolving. We have evidence of doctors in the town in the reign of Charles I, though at this stage medical training in its later sense did not exist. In the late 17th century it was a Warrington apothecary

(a chemist who also dispensed medical advice) to whom the pitiful victims of a mining accident at Whiston turned for help – he gave them drugs and ointments for their wounds at cost price, but then found they were so poor they could not pay his bills.

The professional men and their families had, like the leading merchants, lived close to Market Gate, in the heart of the town. In the late 18th century they began to move out towards the edge, to new houses at the far end of Winwick Street and Bewsey Street and the quiet backwater of Church Street. But industry and pollution, dirt and noise quickly invaded those areas and from the 1850s onwards there was a mass migration to the new exclusive developments in Cairo Street, Bold Street, Springfield Street and, above all, Palmyra Square, laid out in the 1850s. By 1900 the professionals were moving out much further, to the gentle leafy hillsides on the Cheshire side of the river. Then, as Stockton Heath grew, with semi-detached Edwardian villas and those large residences in private grounds on London Road, up the hill south of the canal bridge, so Palmyra Square lost its cachet. The houses remained as surgeries and offices, but the doctors and the lawyers who worked there now lived out of town and commuted in daily. Other large houses became small private schools or were divided into flats. The trend continued almost to the present day, so that now the brass plates of legal firms and accountancy practices adorn almost all the front doors around the square and adjacent streets.

The teaching profession has played a key role in Warrington's development. Historians have frequently considered the greatest might-have-been of Warrington's history, the remarkable flourishing of Warrington Academy and its 'higher education' role in the 1760s and 1770s – a time when there were only two universities in England and Nonconformists and Dissenters were denied access to these. The Academy attracted hundreds of students and also, as teachers, some of the greatest theologians, scientists and literary scholars of the mid-18th century. It could easily have evolved into a university and it is sad indeed that this failed to happen, despite early promise, but its long-term influence was considerable. As a result of the Academy Warrington, which already had the Boteler

William Beamont was a solicitor by profession and the architect of Warrington's Borough Charter granted in 1847. He was the town's first mayor in 1847-8 and helped to set up the new borough's structure of local government.

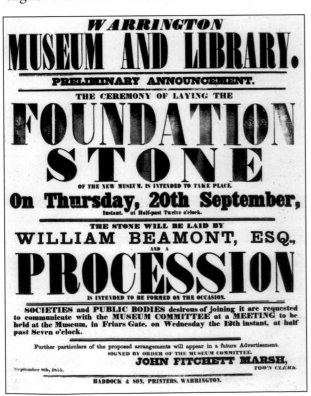

In 1848 Warrington had created the first combined public museum and library in the country. By 1855 the original temporary premises had proved too small and William Beamont, former mayor and keen local historian, laid the foundation stone of the present building.

*Charles Madeley
succeeded to the new
position of museum
curator at Warrington in
1874. In 1848 the Museum
Committee had specified
that the curator should be:
'A person of good educa-
tion and address and
competent to prepare, with
taste and skill, and to keep
in preservation specimens
in every department of
natural history. He will be
required also to act as
librarian, and to have the
general care and manage-
ment of the museum and
library; to which his whole
time will be devoted. He
will be required to live on
the premises, where he will
live rent free, and will have
coal and gas found for him
and a salary of 50 guineas
a year. A married man
without children will be
preferred.'
Madeley served the
institution until his death
in 1920, organising and
cataloguing the collections
and stressing the educa-
tional role of the museum.
He also played a major
role in the development of
his profession nationally
by serving as president of
both the Museum and
Library Associations.*

*The Large Art Gallery of
Warrington Museum is
pictured here just after its
completion in 1877. The
gallery had been funded by
public subscription to
house the work of local
sculptor John Warrington
Wood, whose winged
statue* The Archangel
Michael killing Satan *was
specially created for the
venue.*

grammar school, developed a vigorous and active cultural life which carried on into the 19th century. Later in the Victorian period the teaching profession began to emerge, as more rigorous standards of training were applied. Though Warrington's educational record was poor, there were shining exceptions. In 1838, for example, a non-denominational school was founded by the Nonconformists in Newton Street and it soon developed into the People's College, receiving glowing praise from the government's schools inspectors. In 1839 the Diocese of Chester founded St Elphin's College, intended for the educa-tion of 'the daughters of clergymen and the training of young persons as elemen-tary schoolmistresses'. But, like the Academy, this institution failed to reach its promise and potential, and it later moved to Liverpool.

There are currently 11 banks and seven building societies with branches in Warrington town centre and other branches in Stockton Heath (four), Padgate (two), Penketh (two), Culcheth (four) and Birchwood and Orford , a distribution which closely reflects the relative commercial importance of these local centres in the outer parts of the borough. Some of these go back to the 18th century, when the first banking companies were established in Manchester, Liverpool and other leading provincial centres. The small banking concerns in country towns and centres such as Warrington were eventually taken over by larger regional and national giants, and in the post-war period the number of banks shrank to a mere handful, but the continuity remains. The most famous of Warrington's banks was Parr & Co, founded in 1788 by Joseph Parr, a sugar refiner, Thomas Lyon, brewer and sugar refiner, and Walter Kerfoot, solicitor. The bank which they opened, at 7 Winwick Street, remained purely local for many years – after 75 years it only had branches in Warrington itself, Runcorn and St Helens. However, in 1865 it became a public company and then began to expand, with over 40 branches in Cheshire and Lancashire by 1890. The company opened a London office in 1896 and in 1918 became one of the constituents of the National Provincial Bank, which in turn formed half of the National Westminster created in 1971. More recently Warrington has been recognised as an ideal location for regional and sub-regional offices of financial institutions, so that there are, for example, the

National Westminster Bank's business centre and corporate business centre in its Winwick Street building (where Parr's Bank was founded 230 years ago).

How important were the professions in late Victorian Warrington? In 1891 the legal profession employed 56 people in the borough, the clergy accounted for another 43, there were 78 people in medicine, and in education a total of 300 teachers and administrators. These numbers do not seem large – all the professions put together were outnumbered by the workers at the Whitecross wireworks, for example – but the professions held a power much greater than their numerical presence would indicate. During the 20th century the numbers of professional people have grown extremely quickly. There are far more people involved, and the percentage of the total workforce engaged in this sector has risen sharply. If we take a wide definition of 'professional', to include local and central government administration, for example, the percentage has risen from roughly 5 per cent of the workforce in 1891 to about 20 per cent today. It is a dramatic change – and its visual impact is considerable, too. Just as Palmyra Square was a clearly-defined professional enclave in the 1870s and 1880s, so those offices buildings at Birchwood and other developments of the last 25 years, in the leafy outskirts of the town amid car-parks and boulevards, are occupied by professional firms. And their workers, too, commute in from Cheshire and the villages.

John Warrington Wood was one of a number of local men who had made a name for themselves as artists from the mid-19th century. Together with painters Luke Fildes, Henry Woods and James Charles he won international acclaim for his work. Luke Fildes went on to illustrate the works of Charles Dickens before painting popular works like The Doctor *which now hangs in the Tate Gallery, and the Coronation portrait of King Edward VII.*

The contemporary popularity of Luke Fildes' painting The Doctor *had emphasised the growing respect for a profession which had developed with the advances in medical science in the 19th century. Here the stark ward of Warrington Fever hospital in Aikin Street stands ready to receive isolation cases. In the early 1890s Warrington was the scene of a major outbreak of smallpox, probably originating from the navvies building the Manchester Ship Canal. The insanitary conditions found in the courtyards of the poorer classes who both lived and worked in crowded conditions caused other fevers which filled the reports of the new medical officer of health in the early 20th century. It needed the impact of national legislation on public health and housing and the introduction of the welfare state before conditions improved.*

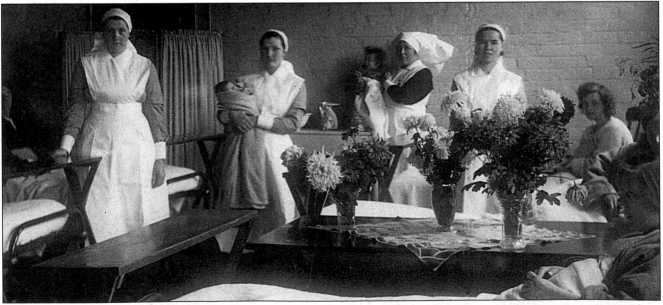

The cheerless surroundings of the maternity ward of Warrington's General Hospital in 1936 before the hospital was taken into the post-World War Two reforms which created the National Health Service. The starched headdress of the authority figure in the background reflected the rigid hierarchy of the nursing profession at the time and a less enlightened attitude to the patients, where mothers who had suffered a still birth had the agony of remaining on the ward with the more fortunate nursing mothers.

The staff of Evelyn Street School poses for an official photograph before World War One. Primly dressed in high-necked blouses and demure long skirts they are ready to instill the 3Rs of Reading (W)riting and (A)rithmetic into their charges. Upon their marriage they would be compelled to give up their profession to bring up their own charges and many remained spinsters to continue with their careers.

The staff of Bolton Council School is captured on an official photograph of 1922. The dresses of the younger members might be looser but the classroom discipline was still rigidly maintained. Warrington's council schools had similar interiors with high windows, two coloured tiles, sparse wall charts and it seems the inevitable aspidistra.

*The old Boteler Grammar School on School Brow, pictured here in
1905, was a male dominated world based on a classical education.
Francis Stansfield, a contemporary pupil, recalled the teachers'
authority: "The masters' desks were more like thrones. The masters
stood at their respective desks, each one of them gowned, with his
mortar board on his desk. Also on his desk lay his cane, a symbol of
his authority as potent as the Speaker's mace...These old walls reeked
of tradition."*

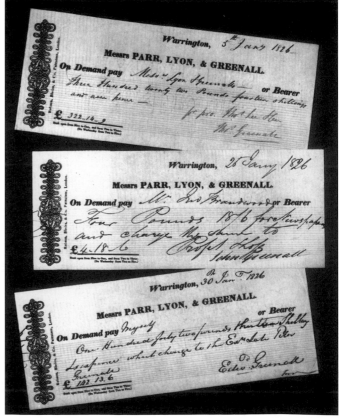

Early 19th-century cheques issued by Parr, Lyon and Greenall's Bank.

Building Public Services

IN 1820, when George IV came to the throne, Warrington had no police, fire service, piped water, gas supply, refuse collection, street cleaning, street lighting, drains or sewers, public transport or public health provision. By 1901, when his niece Victoria died, the town had all these and many other services besides. It had been transformed by the efforts of the public authorities, and by an enormous expenditure of ratepayers' and taxpayers' money, into a modern community with clean water, efficient sewers, reliable law and order enforcement, gas supplies on tap, medical facilities and clean, well-lit streets. The borough council owned the gasworks and waterworks, was building a new electric tramway system, maintained the roads and bridges and the markets, employed a medical officer of health and ran a police force and fire brigade. To the Warrington citizen of 1820 this was impossible to imagine. To the Warringtonian of 1901 it was completely unremarkable. That was one of the real revolutions in the history not just of this town, but of every other in England.

These changes were not easily achieved. Every one generated controversy, sometimes vocal and heated. Every change involved spending money and many were opposed to the changes because of cost and interference in private concerns and individual action. Gradually, the changes were pushed through and life in the town improved as a result. Each produced new employment opportunities, and groups of workers emerged in areas central to the well-being of the community as a whole. Take the example of policing. In 1820 Warrington had no security force apart from a handful of elderly men who on dark nights, often reputed to be the worse for drink, watched the town's streets. In 1900, by contrast, there was a professional borough force which, with its administrative staff, employed a total of 61 people and provided a comprehensive cover for the entire town. The police force, created in 1820, had a chequered early career but by 1847, when it was taken over by the borough council, was properly organised. It was able to deal with matters as diverse as the brawling and fighting between the English and Irish in the town in the 1850s and 1860s and the huge increase in theft and lawlessness

One of Warrington's earliest public servants was the local bellman, or town crier, dressed in his navy frock coat, trimmed with red lapels. As more people learned to read and the town's newspapers flourished his role as public announcer became redundant and the office was phased out in 1902.

On 20 February 1896, Cockhedge Mill was badly damaged by this fire which needed the attention of 17 firemen and both the town's steam fire engines. An earlier fire at the mill in 1872 had revealed the inadequacies of Warrington's fire brigade in dealing with a major industrial blaze. The oil-soaked wooden floors of the mill and highly-inflammable cotton within had swiftly fed the flames. The firemen's ladders and hoses were not long enough to reach the site of the fire and those pumping the manual engines succumbed to their liquid intake supplied by the local inns. The fire was finally brought under control thanks to the efforts of a steam fire engine brought by train from Manchester but not before the mill was gutted. Many months of unemployment followed for the cotton operatives and the incident eventually led to improvements in the borough's fire service provision.

which accompanied the building of the Ship Canal in the 1890s. What could the little band of elderly men have done then!

The fire brigade, too, was formed as a result of the early 19th century changes. Before 1828 the town had six separate private fire engines, each operated by an insurance company and only attending fires in buildings insured by that firm. From 1828 there was a town brigade, staffed by volunteers and reservists. Although this was taken over by the new borough council in 1847 it was many more years before a full-time professional service operated, and fire-fighting still depended on the efforts of the volunteer citizens of the town. In the 20th century

Surrounded by the inevitable crowd of small boys Warrington's two Merryweather steam fire engines are harnessed ready for action. Purchased in 1880 Major cost £463 whilst Captain cost £520 in 1894. The horses were borrowed from local owners who were paid a retaining fee plus 5s (25p) an hour for a fire.

the borough brigade played a heroic part in tackling the massive fires in blitzed cities such as Liverpool and Manchester, and was eventually amalgamated with the county fire service as central government imposed reorganisation in the post-war period.

By the early 20th century Warrington people could turn on the tap and get clean fresh water, light the gas at the cooker or the lamp, or even press a switch and illuminate the room with electric light. Some of them could flush the toilet and not worry about the next stages! Others, who still used the tub toilets out in the backyard, knew that at regular intervals the 'night-soil' men would be along to empty the tubs and take away the contents in a wagon. Their grandparents, back in the reign of George III, were fetching water from the well, lighting smoky tapers to give light, cooking on an open fire, and dumping household waste and night-soil on an open midden or into the brook. That progress was achieved by the workers in the borough's services and the public utilities, provided in the mid-Victorian period. The waterworks at Appleton and Winwick, the gasworks at Mersey Street, the men who maintained the sewers and took away the refuse – these were all part of civilised urban living and the town depended on them heavily. Their jobs may not have been glamourous (in some cases they were definitely unglamorous) and they do not figure much in the photographic record or accounts of the history of the Victorian town, but they were crucial to the efficient operation of every service. They were essential to the increasingly comfortable daily lives of Warrington citizens – and their successors, 100 years on, are just as essential.

There are all sorts of other services and utilities. For instance, the first records of

Warrington's fire brigade proudly poses outside their Queen Street headquarters in the late 1890s. Superintendent Turner senior stands to the right of the ladder. Warrington's highly-combustible factories were under the protection of this crew of 15 part-time firemen, two steam fire- engines and an escape ladder. Brass-buttoned sturdy uniforms, brass helmets, leather boots and belts provided their only safety equipment. All the men carry keys to open the covers of the street hydrants and reach the town's erratic water supply.

Superintendent Frank Turner junior upheld the family tradition by succeeding his father at the helm of the Warrington fire brigade in 1914. Together the two served the brigade for 101 years. His shiny helmet would later be relegated to ceremonial use and fire brigades learnt by bitter experience the dangers caused by a brass helmet making contact with a dangling electric cables in a burning building.

Samuel Andrews, the new PC 38, joined Warrington police force as it moved from the old Irlam Street Bridewell to their new headquarters at Arpley Street in July 1902.

The Thomas Burton, the brigade's new Leyland motor engine, faces its first fire-fighting duties at Bridge Foot in 1914, whilst a local constable controls the watching crowds.

a post office in the town date from the 1630s and by the end of the 17th century, when the Royal Mail had been established, Warrington was the post town for a wide area of south-west Lancashire and north Cheshire. Its key position at the meeting of important trunk roads made it an ideal reception and distribution centre for mail in the 18th century, as the network of fast mailcoach services expanded and operated efficiently to a regular timetable, and in the 21st century precisely the same advantages explain its role as one of the most important points on the national Post Office system. At the more local level, the postal services after 1840, and the introduction of the penny post, involved door-to-door deliveries and collections from the familiar red postbox. The postmen of Warrington represented another everyday service, first developed during Victoria's reign, which is too easily overlooked in considering the town's employment history.

Of all the main employment sectors the one showing the most fluctuations in numbers is the construction and building. Each main project brought large numbers of additional workers to the town, but on a temporary basis. Once the project ended the workers moved on elsewhere. Sometimes the national census was taken just at the point when such a project was under way, as in 1961 when the building of the M6 and Thelwall Viaduct was in progress – but we will have to wait until 2062 to have access to the detailed census returns for that year! However, the Ship Canal was being built when the 1891 census was taken and substantial numbers of labourers are recorded in the area who were working on the project. In the historical record the building trade is poorly represented. Local builders were normally self-employed and few have left any documentary evidence apart from a bills and letterheads. The armies of navvies who came to build canals and railways are known about but not in detail, while there is almost no memory of the men who constructed the mills and factories. Sometimes a photographic record was made of construction projects – the Ship Canal,

because of its vast scale, was a favourite subject for official photographers and amateur cameramen who recorded the enormous disruption which the immense cuttings at Latchford and Walton caused. Earlier, the rebuilding of St Elphin's Church in the late 1850s is the subject of some exceptional early photographs, a rare and valuable record of mid-Victorian construction methods and of the clothing and equipment of labourers, masons and builders 150 years ago. The images taken just before World War One, showing the rebuilding of the corner of Buttermarket Street and Bridge Street, reveal that time-honoured methods were still in use – rickety wooden scaffolding and perilously-placed ladders, horses and carts, wheelbarrows and shovels, picks and spades. In the 1920s the advent of mechanisation for larger-scale construction projects brought about major changes in the way that building was conducted. By the time the new town was being developed in the 1970s, with its expressways, great shopping centres, retail parks, and office buildings, mechanisation and technology played a much more important role – but the building workers and those in the construction trades were just as significant to the town's labour force. In 1991, when the last great phase of new town development was under way, construction accounted for about 6 per cent of the employment in the town.

Charged with the provision of law and order was the Borough's police force which, in 1847, consisted of one constable and four assistants. They were based at the Bridewell (or lock-up) in Irlam Street, close to some of the areas of densest working-class housing and the factories of Cockhedge. By 1854 the force had only risen to nine officers supervising about 24,000 inhabitants, well below the national average. The new Warrington Guardian *campaigned for improvements, asserting: 'There is such excellent railway facilities for travelling to every part of the kingdom that every inducement is held out to rogues to visit us, especially when they know that we have only nine policemen to watch over all our streets, inspect our lodging houses, deliver summonses, attend the petty sessions and assizes, and collect tolls, and these for night duty as well as day.'*

Warrington Borough Police assembled outside the Arpley Street Police Station to commemorate the coronation of Queen Elizabeth II in June 1953.

A growing industrial town with a rapidly increasing population placed increasing demands on the utilities, including gas supply. The Warrington Gas Light and Coke Company had been formed in 1821 to supply coal gas to the area from its Mersey Street Works but by the 1870s could no longer cope with the demand. Warrington Corporation bought out the private company in 1877 and began to increase supply. Alterations began at Mersey Street and this remarkable photograph probably shows the construction of two new gasometers there in the late 1870s. By 1897, however, all gas production had been transferred to a new site at Longford.

Use Electricity.

THE SILENT SERVANT.
ALWAYS READY.
NEVER VARIES.

Saves more than it Costs.

Lighting, Heating, Cooking, Washing, Ironing, &c.

By the 1930s electricity was beginning to replace gas as the main power source, both in the home and for industry. Warrington Corporation had been authorised to supply electricity in 1898 and as this trade advert of the 1930s shows was marketing it as an energy-efficient service.

A council employee empties the drains off Winwick Road early in the last century. This kind of poorly-paid employment was often undertaken by injured industrial workers, as Arthur Shelmerdine recalls: "My father was a boilermaker at Pearson and Knowles and he had his eye knocked out with a rivet. That was his start in married life. He'd only been married a fortnight. He had to finish then. There was no compensation. He didn't get a penny, not even a job. He had to get a job on the Corporation and he could only do that casual because there was so many wanting jobs. It was two years before he got taken on regular and then his wages had only gone to a pound a week. They put him brushing the gutters and he got that efficient they put him emptying the grids with a scoop. He used to take the top off and scoop all the stuff off. For that he got a few bob more."

By 1900 Warrington Corporation was beginning to increase its range of responsibilities by taking over the roles of a number of private companies and, in the process, becoming itself a major employer in the town. In 1902 the privately-owned horse-drawn buses were replaced by Warrington Corporation Tramways. The first tram ran on the Latchford route on 21 April 1902 and the network was gradually extended. Fares were kept to the minimum for the benefit of the working-class but the routes also encouraged the professional classes to commute from their homes in the southern suburbs to their offices in the town centre. By the time of this photograph in 1927 the days of Chief Inspector Quinn and other long-serving tramway staff were numbered.

Postman 48 delivered to the outer districts of Warrington just before World War One. His knickerbocker trousers and leg bandages (or puttees) also gave protection from hostile dogs on his rounds!

Perhaps one of the least enviable jobs in Warrington fell to the 'night soil' men whose essential role involved disposing of the personal waste of the growing population. Originally they had worked under the control of the splendidly-titled Inspector of Nuisances to spirit away their unwholesome cargo at the dead of night whilst the town's good citizens lay sleeping. Later they ventured out in daylight and the inhabitants had to grow used to the sight (and smells) of the weekly exchange of toilet pails. Warrington was one of the last towns in the north west to retain this insanitary progress and the workmen are seen here one of their last rounds in the 1950s.

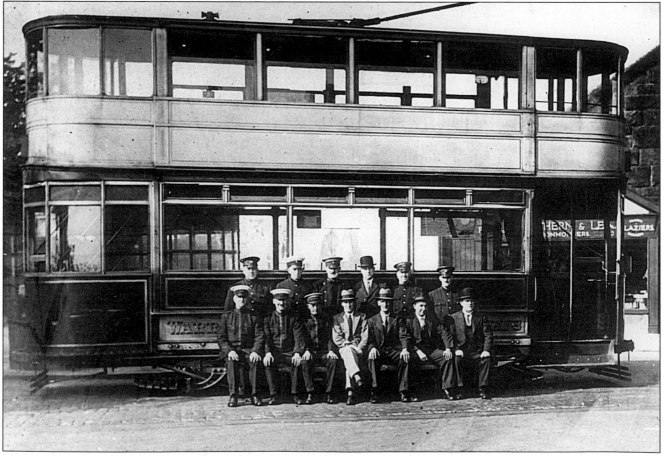

This Latchford tram had reached its terminus and, on 28 August 1935, the last of over 225 million passengers completed their journey on Warrington's trams. Motor buses had already been introduced on some routes in 1913 and now a fleet of new Leyland double-deckers took to Warrington's roads to usher in a new stage of public transport.

In 1908, as Warrington's businesses and offices generated an increased volume of mail, and the picture postcard grew in popularity, a new central post office opened in Springfield Street to cope with the demand.

A new employment opportunity for women came as telephone operators at Warrington's central telephone exchange early in the 20th century. Warrington's industry began to embrace the new system of communications and even a few wealthier private subscribers got connected.

The 'Hello Girls' of Stockton Heath telephone exchange pause briefly in their duties in the early 1960s, supervised by Mary Rimmer on the left. Customers still had to stay on the line to be connected manually but, with the expansion of business and private use, the personal touch eventually gave way to an automated system.

Construction work on the Manchester Ship Canal in the early 1890s brought some of the first cranes and earth-moving equipment to the town and, as the 20th century dawned, major new civil engineering projects brought more employment opportunities for construction workers.

Between 1900 and 1915 a large-scale redevelopment of Bridge Street saw the town's main thoroughfare swarming with builders. The industry was still comparatively labour-intensive, wages were low and health and safety concerns were still a century away.

The rebuilding of Warrington Bridge between 1911 and 1915 saw a much more disciplined approach to civil engineering. New skills could be learnt in the techniques of building with reinforced concrete and Albert Thorne's men brought cranes for the heavier work. Here the first half of the new bridge is being surfaced ready for the official opening by King George V in July 1913.

The building of Warrington's second Mersey crossing at Bridge Foot in the 1990s saw similar scenes to that of the 1913 bridge but the cranes were larger and the wearing of hard hats was just one of the new safety precautions.

The Guardians of History

WE could not have written this book without the people who work in publishing, printing and photography. Since the middle of Victoria's reign the life of Warrington has been recorded by the newspapers, most notably the *Warrington Guardian* which in 2003 celebrates its 150th anniversary as the leading local paper. During that time it has faithfully

Arthur Bennett (2nd from the right) and his staff at the Eagle Printing Works are recorded by Walter Crompton in the early 1900s shortly before the demolition of the premises with the redevelopment of the town centre. This was both a news story and a record of Warrington's heritage commissioned by Bennett for his short-lived magazine called The Dawn. *An accountant by profession, Bennett also campaigned for the development of the town in a way that would preserve its unique heritage. Crompton became the town's first photo-journalist although, within a few years, employees of both the* Warrington Guardian *and the* Warrington Examiner *were able to make use of improved technology to follow suit.*

charted everything that happened in the town and the surrounding villages. If we want to know the date of an event, track down a theme in the town's history, find out what people thought about a burning issue of the day or, more recently, see a contemporary image, we look at the *Warrington Guardian* and the chances are that we will find the evidence, picture, quotation, or description we are seeking. No less valuable for the historian are the advertisements – a marvellous source of information about what people were buying at what prices, where businesses were located, who was selling land and cattle and shoes and ladies' fashions. We can check through columns of births, marriages and deaths; follow the fortunes, good and bad, of any sports team in the town; read about horrible murders and golden weddings, royal visits and sensational robberies, the opening of new roads and the closing of long-established factories. All life is there, and if we go to Warrington Library and look at the newspapers on microfilm we can be lost in the world of the not-so-distant past, remembering events and people or imaging what it must have been like.

That rich and fascinating historical resource (which is also a contemporary and up-to-date source of information as well) gives us a different dimension to the past. We learn about the unofficial history of the town. If we read the council minutes of the 1870s and 1880s, when major new public projects were being undertaken or considered – taking over the gasworks and waterworks, building new streets, opening schools in working-class areas – we find a bland and carefully-phrased version of events, recording the decisions made at the end of the day. But the *Guardian*'s reports of debates in the town council record the speeches which councillors made, with all the jeers and heckling, polite condemnation of the opponents, heated argument about the rights and wrongs of issues … the reality of it all.

Over 150 years ago towns such as Warrington did not usually have a newspaper. This particular town, though, was very early in the field – in the summer of 1756 the Eyre family, who owned a printing press and bookshop, produced a few issues of *Eyre's Weekly Journal* or *The Warrington Advertiser*, one of the very earliest attempts to found a newspaper in a small provincial town. It did not survive and, apart from the very short-lived *Warrington Observer: A Weekly Journal of Literary, Religious and Miscellaneous Information* (summer 1830) and the *Advertiser* (a couple of issues in the spring of 1851), there was nothing until the *Guardian* began publication on 9 April 1853. Thereafter there were dozens of other attempts to found rival papers, some (such as the *Examiner*, published more or less continuously from 1909 to 1959) being more successful than others (the *Warrington Leader* ran only from February to March 1905).

The flourishing of Warrington Academy from 1757 to 1786 was a major incentive to publishing in the town. The Eyre family were the main inspiration behind the project to produce textbooks and academic publications, using the Eyre's Press imprint. Today this is what might be known as a 'university press'

Alexander Mackie, pictured here in 1886, had launched the Warrington Guardian *series of weekly newspapers in 1853. His first editorial laid out his paper's intention: 'To our townspeople we now commit the* Warrington Guardian, *trusting to their efforts, in conjunction with our own, to render the* Guardian *instrumental in promoting the advancement amongst us of knowledge and refinement, and earning for Warrington once more the title to the high character which it bore in former years for intellectual culture and enterprise'. These lofty aims seemed to establish the paper as the natural successor to Eyre's* Warrington Advertiser *at the time in the late 18th century when Warrington styled itself 'the Athens of the North'. His choice of title was also significant and was possibly inspired by his admiration for the radical* Manchester Guardian, *and for many years the paper bore the masthead 'Neutral in all matters Political and Religious'.*

This 1860s photograph is the first local photograph of a compositor at work, showing the painstaking process of typesetting.

and, had Warrington Academy survived to become England's third university, this is surely what the press would have become. Even though that did not happen book publishing remained a significant feature of the town, and in the early 19th century Warrington not only had a private circulating library and a number of learned societies with their own library collections (which together would form the basis of one of Britain's pioneering public libraries in 1848) but it also had a flourishing publishing industry. In the 1891 census there were listed 171 men and 79 women who were engaged in printing, publishing and library work, a figure far higher in relation to the size of population than for comparably-sized cotton towns such as Bury, Rochdale and Burnley.

From the mid-1850s a new attraction appeared on the streets of the town – the new-fangled photographer with his camera and cumbersome cases, lenses, tripods and other equipment. Warrington has a particularly fine collection of very early photographic images, including some of the first outdoor pictures, everyday street scenes, from any English town. These have priceless historical value – the images of St Elphin's Church being rebuilt in the late 1850s, the fair in Church Street (abolished in 1859) and, perhaps most remarkable of all, the laying of the foundation stone of the museum in 1855, have few parallels. From this time onwards the photographers seem to have popped up whenever and wherever anything interesting was happening. Thus, Arthur Bennett, the campaigning conservationist councillor of the years after 1900, appears in all sorts of images –

By the 1920s the Warrington Guardian *was using the latest linotype machines and printing presses at its Sankey Street headquarters.*

standing perilously balanced on the rafters of a historic building being demolished, watching work on road-widening in progress, opening the new council houses at Bewsey. We have images of Warrington people famous and unknown, barefoot children and toiling workers, busy shoppers and passengers standing on railway station platforms, labourers digging the canal and farmers guiding plough-horses. We see King George V and Queen Mary outside the Town Hall in 1913; GIs at Burtonwood and at town centre dance halls; people staring appalled and stunned at the huge crater in the field outside the Thames Board works after the 1940 air raid; and children and their teachers sitting in neat rows for school photographs. Without the photographer our knowledge of the town, its people and its life would be so much less, as it inevitably is for the centuries which stretch back before the 1850s. We should be ever grateful for their work.

By contrast the Guardian's *chief reporters still preferred more traditional methods to compose their stories.*

By the time the Warrington Guardian *celebrated its 125th birthday in 1978, linotype had given way to the latest electronic typesetting equipment, which still seems a world away from the revolutionary impact of the computer on journalism into the 21st century.*

When the Warrington Guardian *first appeared on the town's streets in 1853, photography was still in its infancy but, as the* Guardian *was busy filing news stories, Thomas Birtles was soon busy creating a visual record of Warrington and its citizens. This early 1860s studio portrait is possibly the first photograph of Birtles himself with the cumbersome photographic equipment of the day.*

Not all local weddings made major news stories but when Susannah Greenall of Walton Hall married her cousin Cyril in 1898 both the Warrington Guardian *and Thomas Birtles were on hand to record the event. This is hardly surprising in retrospect since Sir Gilbert Greenall (second from left) had a substantial financial stake in the newspaper and, like Birtles, was a major figure in the local Conservative Party.*

A studio portrait of Councillor Thomas Birtles who had become a prominent local Conservative politician as well as being accorded membership of the Royal Photographic Society in recognition of his professional work. He had been commissioned by Sir Edward Leader Williams to record the construction of the Manchester Ship Canal and Warrington Borough Council had also entrusted his studio with the task of documenting the redevelopment of Warrington's town centre and the building of the new Warrington Bridge.

An interior view of Birtles' Legh House Studio off Sankey Street in 1908, which was said to be 'completely equipped with all the latest appliances, and provided with unsurpassed northern light'. Birtles' advertisements also proclaimed: 'His productions in every branch of photographic work, in enlargements and miniatures, in children's and animal photographs, in groups, interiors, landscapes, machinery and architectural photographs... are faultless works of art in arrangement, tone and finish'. Birtles was assisted by two of his daughters and by his son, John Edward Birtles, who continued the business until the mid-1950s. Many of the finest photographs in the collections held by Warrington's Library, Museum and Archive Service have originated from Birtles' studio and form an invaluable record for local historians.

This photograph taken by Walter Crompton in the early 1900s documents several important facets of Warrington's history. These premises in Friars' Gate had been the first home of Warrington's Museum and Library in 1848; the building was currently the headquarters of the Warrington branch of the Independent Labour Party at a time when the movement was still struggling to establish itself; it is also a record of the location of Charles Cooke's photographic studio and lastly, but of equal importance, it records the everyday clothing and activities of local people like the lamp-lighter.

A world away from Birtles' plush studio was the tin shack occupied by H.E. Tonge at Latchford. Apart from taking less expensive portraits of local people his photographs of everyday events also found their way into the Warrington Examiner or were sold as picture postcards.

The Decline of
Traditional Employment

AT TIMES, in the 1970s and 1980s, it might have seemed that hardly a week went by without the *Warrington Guardian* reporting the closure of a family firm, job losses at a major plant or, not infrequently, its total closure.

Warrington's employment structure and the working lives of its people were at the mercy of the world economy. That was not in itself new – most of the heavy industries which had grown in the town in the century and a half from 1760 were responding to the Industrial Revolution, to the development of worldwide markets (for example, in wire products for agriculture and industrial processing) and to the inexorable rise of the consumer age. But the major difference was that, whereas in the 19th century Britain was the world's leading industrial power and so it supplied its manufactured products to a global market, in the last 100 years strong competition, and then the rise of new industrial powers such as Germany, Japan and the United States, ended that role. British industries of all sorts faced ever-greater difficulties in selling their products, simply because other countries also produced the goods. At the same time, the accelerating pace of technical innovation and technological change meant that industry itself was forced to restructure or collapse. There were other challenges and problems. The word 'rationalisation' – and its later euphemistic alternative 'downsizing' – became commonplace, pointing to (or sometimes concealing) wholesale closures of industrial plant. Takeovers and mergers inevitably led to closure and job losses, while firms, with familiar names that had become household words, and which had

The last billet of steel emerges form Number 4 Rolling Mill in March 1986.

Shunting into the sidings of history at Winwick junction in 1962, which was shortly to become Winwick Quay industrial estate.

for many decades been associated with one product moved, because of the pressures and temptations of new fields of investment and activity, into very different spheres.

Such problems even affected industries which were only 50 or 60 years old. Take packaging, for example – the production of corrugated cardboard, boxes and cartons continued into the 1990s, when it began to experience major economic problems which stemmed from world-wide changes in the market and were highlighted by takeovers and the globalisation of production. Thames Board (renamed Thames Case) was eventually acquired by the multinational giant Unilever, whose own close connections with Warrington have already been considered, but eventually closed. The Alliance Box Company became part of the Irish-based Smurfit Group and the Warrington works ceased operation in the spring of 2002. Yet this industry had only come into its own in the 1920s and 1930s, when it had seemed a sign of a new and bright economic future for Warrington.

Heavy industry was hardest hit and even Warrington's Rugby League team was renamed Warrington Wolves as the wire industry lost its dominance in the town. To the average person elsewhere Rylands was not a name that meant anything, but for a whole section of British industry over 150 years the name was synonymous with Warrington and wire. The closure of the firm, the demolition of the works, and the construction of Sainsbury's superstore on the site somehow symbolised not just a local economic and employment crisis, but also a much wider and more deep-seated message – the failure of British industry in the second half of the 20th century.

More dramatic, and more emotive, was the closure of Greenall's brewery in 1991, with its major impact upon local employment, the landscape of the Wilderspool area and – no less significant – the town's image. Greenall's had been part of Warrington for over 200 years, the Greenall family had been leaders of town society for much of that time, and to the

New employment opportunities arose at the industrial estates created with the development of Warrington New Town.

outside world Greenall's ales were one of the labels by which Warrington was known. The loss of Greenall's was not only potentially a very serious economic blow to Warrington, but was seen by many as a betrayal of 200 and more years of tradition, loyalty and identity.

The closure of factories is only part of the story of decline in traditional employment. The reshaping of the labour force is much less obvious and rarely hits the headlines, but throughout the

Rubery Owen, another old-established Warrington firm reached the end of the road in the mid-1980s.

20th century things were constantly in a state of flux. One such 'invisible' decline was in the railway industry. Though most of the town's railways remain open, the numbers employed are a tiny fraction of the labour force before World War One. Engine sheds have disappeared with diesel and electric traction; freight yards and sidings have either been closed or are operated with a minimal number of staff; and stations no longer have armies of porters, delivery boys and signalmen.

Even more significant was domestic service, one of Warrington's largest categories of employment 100 years ago. Virtually every worker was female and a high proportion were young – 'going into service' was the inevitable destiny of many girls. Warrington had a middle-class large enough to offer substantial employment for daily servants, though there were relatively few live-in maids except in the large private houses of Stockton Heath, Palmyra Square and Grappenhall. By the late 1930s, though, the number of domestic servants was falling fast and in the 1950s the decline became a headlong rush. There were all sorts of contributory factors: servants' wages 100 years ago were notoriously poor

Furnaces at British Steels Bewsey Road Works (formerly Pearson & Knowles) prepare to shut down in 1980.

No hope of an armistice for Armitage & Rigby's Mill as the site was earmarked for redevelopment in the 1980s.

and as, in the 1930s, the wage costs rose to slightly more acceptable levels many middle-class householders gave up the social status of servant-keeping. More important, though, was the advent of a multitude of labour-saving devices such as the vacuum cleaner and the washing machine which made housework less arduous and much cleaner for the housewife. Warrington's own Persil was not insignificant in all this – many servants spent a lot of their working time trying to make the clothes clean, and washing powders could do this at a fraction of the cost and with a lot less trouble. From the 1920s and 1930s houses were increasingly built on the assumption that servants would not be employed – homes were designed to be compact and labour-saving, with wipeable surfaces and gas or electric heating. Domestic service in the old sense was virtually extinct by 1960 and one of the main elements in the old employment structure was gone.

Even in sectors where overall numbers remained fairly constant, the types of jobs changed almost beyond recognition. In retailing, for example, most corner shops closed in the second half of the century, while employment in supermarkets – undreamed of before World War Two – assumed a major significance. The proliferation of offices, new electronic and light industries, and large shops provided a new form of service. Whereas 100 years ago the majority of those involved in what could loosely be described as 'cleaning' were employed in private households, today that sector has been reclassified and many part-time

The looms are silent and only the clamour of shoppers can be heard under the salvaged roof girders of the old mill which were incorporated into the new Cockhedge shopping centre.

jobs for women are in commercial cleaning and related work. The firms which provide office pot-plant maintenance and the staff who clean telephones and computers had no Edwardian equivalent: their emergence as new types of employment is a consequence of the ever-fluid state of the labour market.

Warrington: Where Knowledge Goes to Work

THE decline of traditional industries is familiar theme in any history of Lancashire or of its individual towns. Indeed, it has become a refrain in most histories of modern Britain as a whole. For many places the process was acutely painful and had long-term consequences of unemployment, economic depression, social malaise and environmental deterioration which are all too familiar. Warrington, though, has not only weathered the storms but also emerged in a leading position as an employment and commercial centre, with some extremely impressive economic statistics to highlight its success:

- Warrington receives 10 per cent of all inward investment in the North-West
- The increase in the town's industrial and commercial value in 1998-99 was 4.7 per cent compared with 1 per cent in the region and 1.9 per cent in the UK
- Unemployment rates (currently 1.7 per cent) are not only well below those for the region, but also below those for Cheshire and the country as a whole
- Warrington is the only north-west location in the top 25 'local competitiveness' and 'knowledge-based industries' ratings, ranking with places such as West Sussex and Oxfordshire
- In 1991-2001 it was the second most successful location for employment growth

The growth of new employment sectors has made a huge difference to the town's competitiveness and helped it to overcome the loss of major industries and even to accelerate its growth rate despite those losses. Some of these changes are widespread and have affected every town. For example, if you walk along any of the main streets in Warrington town centre today you see the evidence of the greatest growth industry of our time. The financial sector is now one of the dominant elements in *Warrington at Work* and one of the most important elements in British society. Fifty years ago the presence of the world of finance was relatively modest – there were bank buildings, usually designed in the 1890s or the Edwardian period, the first great age for corporate bank architecture, but little else. Now, we see the plate glass windows of building societies and finance agencies, and in the business parks the financial institutions public and private are to be found. Thousands of people in the borough are employed in this sector and it is a key element in the local economy … yet a century ago it barely existed. Of all the changes in the past 100 years, during the reshaping of *Warrington at Work*, this is perhaps the most profound yet the least obvious. We see the building society premises and we go to the bank but, like the proverbial iceberg, the behind-the-scenes business of money, finance, loans and borrowings, financial management, insurance, exchange and credit is vastly greater than the average member of the public sees.

Other changes are less evenly spread, and Warrington has specialised in the new sectors of electronics, computing, admin-istrative services and institutional operations centres. The town has been able to regenerate itself in business because no one sector has dominated, but unlike some other places with high growth in new sectors this has not been led by the public sector (a reliance on government funding) but market-led because of location, a highly-developed infrastructure and a reservoir of skills and excel-lence on which firms have been able to draw. The town's leaders think in terms, not of 'industrial' and 'services', but in new ways, where the old labels and divisions no longer have relevance.

One of Warrington's pristine new workplaces of the 21st century.

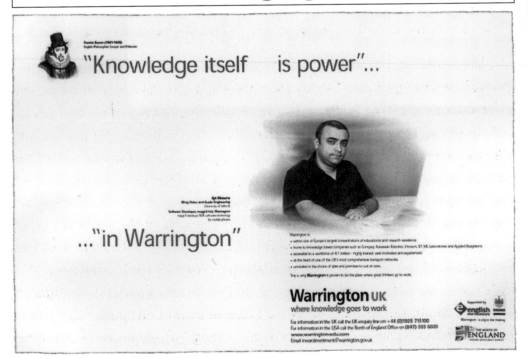

Thus the offices on the science parks may not look like factories but many of them do produce – a new piece of technology such as a microchip which improve and constantly update mobile phones is as much a part of modern business output as a length of wire or a pint of beer in Warrington's traditional industries. Warrington has a flourishing IT sector, including Hewlett Packard which sells its business solutions; Telecom; and Vodafone runs its network switching operation from Birchwood. The nuclear industry was among the pioneers of this type of new approach to production and employment, with BNFL at Risley, but Warrington-based NNC (formerly National Nuclear Computing) markets design safety solutions to the industry worldwide. Birchwood has reinvented itself three times over, changing in only half a century from the Risley munitions factories, via the UK's nuclear research headquarters, to the Business Park which reflects the leading edge of modern technology.

As an example of the new type of business, Hiden Analytical (which employs 60 people at its base at Europa Boulevard on the edge of the Gemini Retail Park) is a global leader in the design and production of exceptionally sophisticated precision scientific instruments. Its main sales areas are the Far East, Europe and the United States. Hiden came to Warrington in 1981 because of its excellent communications, easy access to the research expertise of world-class academic institutions (there are nine major universities within 50 miles of Warrington), its proximity to Manchester Airport, and its impressive availability of factory units. This story could be repeated many times over. The biotechnology sector is well-represented, with Applied Biosystems which has been at Birchwood since the late 1980s, involved with the Celera Discovery System which provides genomic information for researchers, facilitating computer testing of medicines.

Whole new areas of work have emerged as a result of the technological changes – the town's large call centres, and the National Westminster's corporate business centre, are examples. But though the communications are now electronic, the value and importance of the location remains. If we think about the working lives of the Warringtonians who are employed in these new sectors we can see that the changes even from the experience of 30 years ago are dramatic. The working environment has changed almost beyond recognition in that time, but just as significant is the fact that these, like so many others, are not just Warrington businesses but world businesses. In some cases the decisions which control how they operate and what they do are made hundreds or thousands of miles away, in London or Frankfurt or Hong Kong. The financial sector, with its vital importance to the well-being of the town, demonstrates that Warrington is now a place within a vast global network of business and commercial organisation, while the industries based on new technologies work in an environment where the entire world is the market and local and national barriers hardly count at all. A hundred years ago it was possible to look at the employment structure of the town, to list the major firms and businesses working in Warrington, and to say that almost all of them were owned locally, often by people native to the town, and they had deeply-rooted ties with the place, the people and the community. Now that is no longer true. Hardly any major Warrington businesses are a Warrington company in origin, and few are now Warrington-controlled. If, 50 years ago, people had foreseen this, they might well have been dismayed and shocked, but we should not make too much of this, for the same lesson applies to just about every other important English town – but it is a crucial dimension to the modern economic structure of each one.

The last great piece in the jigsaw of Warrington at Work as we know it is now being put in place. The massive Omega development, now under way, will further boost the town's economic base, diversify its employment and generate jobs and wealth. Omega is one of the largest single business and industrial development projects ever undertaken in the United Kingdom. With the potential for almost three-quarters of a million square metres of commercial floorspace, the likely creation of at least 12,000 jobs, and a total cost in excess of £1 billion, it is certain to become a major economic focus not just for the district around but also for northern England as a whole. Historians in the future will see the completion of Omega, scheduled for 2010, as one of the most significant events in the 2,000 year history of the town, while those looking at north-west England will identify it as a landmark in the region's economic history.

Warrington, faced with exactly the same changes in the world as every other place, has been so much more successful than most in meeting the challenge. In this book we have tried to show how diverse and varied such lives have been in the past and are in the present day. Working life for a lot of the citizens of the town in the past was spent behind the counter, or in the classroom, or on the horse and cart, or at the clerk's desk or cashier's window, or standing at the market stall. For others it meant child employment in factories and workshops, herculean efforts of manual labour in ironworks or wireworks, or the delicate operation of packing and labelling fragrant soaps at Crosfield's. Today it might be spent gazing at a computer screen in an office building at Birchwood, fingers flickering across a keyboard, or serving in Weatherspoon's, or driving a taxi, or pushing goods trolleys in Marks and Spencer. All these and countless other jobs make up the working lives of Warrington and its people and in this book at least part of their story has been told.

Index